PATIENT ZERO

SOLVING THE MYSTERIES OF DEADLY EPIDEMICS

MARILEE PETERS

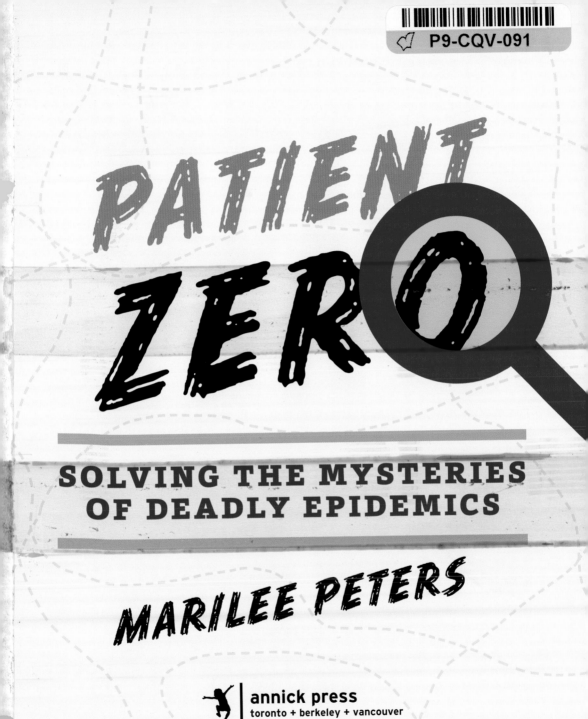

annick press
toronto + berkeley + vancouver

TO MY CHILDREN AND EDITORIAL ADVISORS, OLIVIA AND JACKSON, FOR FEARLESSLY OFFERING THEIR OPINIONS DURING THE WRITING OF THIS BOOK— AND FOR BEING RIGHT

© 2014 Marilee Peters

Fourth printing, December 2019

Cover illustration (doctor with medical mask): © Lightspring / Shutterstock.com
All artwork © lineartestpilot / Shutterstock.com unless otherwise noted.
Page 3 (road and hospital) © Diego Schtutman / Shutterstock.com; pp. 4–5
(medical equipment) © Panom / Shutterstock.com; p. 59 & 85 (doctor & nurse)
© grmarc / Shutterstock.com; p. 121 (microscope) © sparkstudio / Shutterstock.
com; p. 122 (name tag) © David Burden / Shutterstock.com; p. 124 (straw huts)
© TheBlackRhino / Shutterstock.com; p. 157 (map) © Volina / Shutterstock.com;
p. 166 (author photo) © Melanie Port.

Edited by Barbara Pulling
Copyedited by Pam Robertson
Proofread by Linda Pruessen
Designed by Natalie Olsen/Kisscut Design

Annick Press Ltd.

We acknowledge the support of the Canada Council for the Arts, the Ontario
Arts Council, and the participation of the Government of Canada/la participation du gouvernement du Canada for our publishing activities.

ONTARIO ARTS COUNCIL
CONSEIL DES ARTS DE L'ONTARIO
an Ontario government agency
un organisme du gouvernement de l'Ontario

Cataloging in Publication
Peters, Marilee, 1968–, author
Patient zero : solving the mysteries of deadly epidemics / Marilee Peters.

Includes bibliographical references and index.
ISBN 978-1-55451-670-4 (pbk.).—ISBN 978-1-55451-671-1 (bound)

1. Epidemics—History—Juvenile literature.   2. Communicable diseases—
History—Juvenile literature.   I. Title.

RA653.5.P48 2014   j614.4'9   C2014-900436-2

Published in the U.S.A. by Annick Press (U.S.) Ltd.
Distributed in Canada by University of Toronto Press.
Distributed in the U.S.A. by Publishers Group West.

Printed in China

Visit us at: **www.annickpress.com**
Visit Marilee Peters at: **www.marileepeters.ca**

Also available in e-book format.
Please visit **www.annickpress.com/ebooks.html**
for more details.

CONTENTS

INTRODUCTION

A RACE AGAINST TIME

With a buzz and a crackle, the pilot's voice came over the intercom. "Buckle up, please. We'll be beginning our descent in just a few minutes."

As the plane emerged from the clouds, Dr. Shannon McKay stared out her window at the city below. Gradually the grid of streets came into focus, revealing tiny buildings, houses, trees, and lawns. Then the airport runway rushed up to meet them, and the plane bumped to a stop. The doors opened. Shannon's stomach, which had been churning with excitement for the entire trip, clenched with fear. What was out there?

It was her first field assignment, and she'd been sent to this remote city along with a small team of scientists to investigate a recent outbreak of disease. Their mission: to identify the cause of the epidemic and stop it before it spread beyond the city's borders. Reports from the region had been confused but urgent. Doctors at the local hospital weren't sure what the disease was—while some thought it might be plague, others argued it was a new virus, never seen before. All they knew for sure was that the disease was deadly, and it was spreading fast.

The airport was chaotic, crowded with people clamoring to get on a flight, any flight, and escape from the city before they became infected. As Shannon and the other scientists pushed their way through the throng, Shannon scanned strangers' faces warily for signs of illness.

At the hospital, the doctor in charge was gray with exhaustion. Beds and stretchers loaded with moaning patients packed the narrow hallways.

"It all started a week ago," the head doctor told the scientists. "At first it was just a couple of people. We couldn't identify the illness, but we weren't too worried. Then more and more people started showing up with the same symptoms. We've run out of beds, and the morgue is full now too."

The investigation team huddled in a small office to go over their plans. They had to gather information quickly while doing everything they could to control the spread of the disease.

They'd need to close the airport, establish isolation wards and quarantines, collect data on the number of infected victims, and start laboratory testing to determine the cause of the outbreak.

"McKay, I want you to handle patient interviews," the lead investigator ordered. "Find out what people were doing before they got sick. Where did they go? What did they eat? Who did they come in contact with? Take one of the local translators with you. And we need to figure out who was the first person to get sick—who's our Patient Zero? The answers are out there, we just have to find them."

Shannon nodded. Quickly, she zipped up her biohazard suit and grabbed her laptop, ready to head out into the hospital wards. There was no time to lose.

The thought of getting caught up in a massive epidemic frightens a lot of people, and for good reason. The Black Death, cholera, yellow fever, AIDS: throughout human history millions of people have died in epidemics—far more than have died in wars or other disasters.

Across the world today, our defenders against epidemics are the scientists who strive to unravel the mysteries behind these deadly outbreaks. They search for clues that can tell us how a disease outbreak started, how it spreads, and what puts people at risk of getting sick. We call these scientists who work on understanding and stopping disease outbreaks *epidemiologists*.

Like detectives, epidemiologists travel to the "scene of the crime" to look for clues when a disease strikes. They ask lots of questions, look for witnesses, talk to the victims, sniff out facts that may have been overlooked, and then assemble the evidence. Working with the latest technology in special laboratories, they also use high-level scientific skills to uncover hidden connections and test their theories.

National and international organizations such as the U.S. Centers for Disease Control (CDC), the World Health Organization (WHO), and the Public Health Agency of Canada continuously monitor disease reports from around the world, ready at a moment's notice to send teams of epidemiologists to the latest disease hotspot. But epidemiology (pronounced epeh-dee-mee-ol-o-gy) hasn't always been as sophisticated as it is today. In fact, it's only thanks to the lonely, dangerous work of a few dedicated doctors and scientists that we now know how to prevent or cure some of the most deadly diseases in history.

Diseases like plague, cholera, and typhoid fever. Those names can still strike fear into our hearts, even today. The scientists who unraveled the medical mysteries behind these illnesses faced a terrifying prospect: they were risking their lives to fight diseases that killed thousands of people every year. They needed to be courageous, and very determined; all too often, no one believed their crazy theories. They were ignored, laughed at, sometimes even fired from their jobs. But they kept searching for answers, putting the pieces of the puzzles of epidemics together. Today, millions of people owe their lives to the work of such early epidemiologists.

And the fight against infectious disease isn't over yet. Epidemics and pandemics continue to threaten the world. As our populations grow, and as technology, climate change, and wars change the way we live all around the globe, tracking and stopping disease outbreaks is more important than ever.

It's easy to see why. Today, we live in a global village, and an outbreak from anywhere in the world can arrive on our doorsteps in a matter of hours. Just imagine, for instance, what could happen if a deadly new disease were to emerge in one of the world's biggest cities and major transport hubs: a city like Tokyo, New York, Shanghai, or London. Simply by stepping onto a plane, infected victims could spread the epidemic around the country, and even around the world, in a fraction of the time it would take to bring international medical aid. That's the kind of scenario that keeps today's epidemiologists ever on the alert, ready to track down the source of the next killer epidemic.

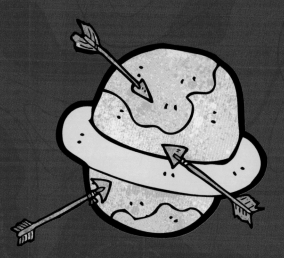

PANICKING OVER PANDEMICS

When is an outbreak an epidemic, and when is it a pandemic?

When the number of cases of a disease in a region is clearly higher than normal, it's an epidemic. Once doctors start reporting an unusual number of patients, public health authorities may declare that there is an epidemic underway. They'll alert the media so people can take precautions against the disease. Hopefully, it doesn't go much further.

If it does, it may become a pandemic: a worldwide epidemic that infects a large number of people over a very wide area, in different countries and regions of the globe. The World Health Organization monitors disease outbreaks, and when cases are reported in three or more countries, it's officially a pandemic.

A pandemic can be deadly, like AIDS, the Black Death, or Spanish flu. Or it can be milder, like the 2009 swine flu pandemic, which was fatal to less than 1 percent of patients. But when we see the word pandemic in a headline, we panic!

1

LONDON'S DREADFUL VISITATION

THE GREAT PLAGUE EPIDEMIC OF 1665

The rat looked dead. Goodwoman Phillips nudged it with her toe to be sure. It didn't move.

She bent down, pinched its tail between her thumb and forefinger, and lifted the rat up so it dangled limply before her face. "Come into my kitchen and die on my clean floor, will you?" she said menacingly to the little corpse. "We'll see about that, you dirty beast." Goodwoman noticed with disgust that fleas were still jumping in the rat's coarse black fur—clearly it hadn't been dead for long. Probably killed by the cold: this winter had been the coldest anyone in London could remember, and more than rats were dying during the freezing nights.

She opened the door and swung the rat by its tail, flinging it as far from the house as she could. It landed with a thud in the gutter. Good riddance to bad rubbish, thought Goodwoman Phillips, and she turned back inside, dusting her hands briskly on her skirts, ready to begin making breakfast.

She thought no more about the rat that day or the next. She was a busy woman, with a husband and sons to feed and clothe. And for a poor family like hers, living outside the walls of London in the rough and tumble parish of St. Giles in the Fields, food and clothes were often hard to come by. Worse, with this winter's dreadful cold, they needed more fuel than usual for the fire. Goodwoman feared that the extra expense would mean Christmas, just a few days away, would be a lean and dismal holiday this year.

Goodwoman Phillips was right to worry about Christmas. There would be no celebrating in her home. As that dark December day wore on, her head began aching, and her back and limbs pained her so much that she could hardly stand. At first she tried to ignore it, but then fever and chills set in. By evening she was shaking so badly that she was forced to take to her bed. She lay in a daze, trying not to moan.

SIGNS IN THE SKY

Goodwoman Phillips didn't want to worry her husband and family, but they could plainly see how ill she was. Her sons sat by her bedside, trying to distract her with stories of the things they'd heard and seen in the city of London, where they picked up what work they could, fetching and carrying for tradesmen. All of London, they told her, was buzzing with rumors and speculation about the meaning of the dreadful sign that had been spotted in the night sky. Since November, a comet had been seen flaring across the heavens every clear night. It foretold evil ahead, everyone agreed, but what would the awful event be?

According to the latest rumor circulating through the city, the comet was a sign that England's king, Charles II, did not have God's favor. As a result, terrible punishments would be unleashed on the country.

At this, Goodwoman Phillips raised her head weakly from the pillow. "My mother always said that plague follows a coronation. Charles has been on the throne four years, and in that time England has had no plague. Perhaps the sign in the sky foretells that God is sending the plague to visit this city again." Then, as a fresh wave of fever shook her, Goodwoman Phillips's thoughts drifted. She stared blankly out at the stars glinting through her window. Her sons crept away, leaving her to rest. Soon she was tossing in a restless, feverish sleep.

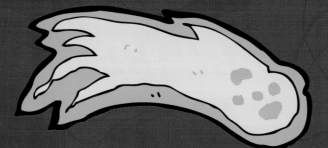

CALAMITY
FROM THE SKY

"These Blazeing Starrs! Threaten the World with Famine, Plague, & Warrs. To Princes, Death; to Kingdoms, many Crises; to all Estates, inevitable Losses!"

John Gadbury, an English astrologer, delivered this terrifying prediction in a pamphlet he published in early 1665. It was his interpretation of the comet's appearance in the skies above London. The whole city was riveted by the nightly phenomenon, first spotted in late November of 1664. There was general agreement that the comet was a bad omen. But of what?

Predictions abounded of terrible wars, famines, and diseases to come. One writer warned that the comet would be the cause of "a MORTALITY which will bring MANY to their Graves."

We know today that the epidemic of plague that engulfed the city the following summer had much more to do with dirty and overcrowded living conditions that brought people into close contact with rats and fleas than it did with any astronomical event. But for the people of London, the plague and the comet were both mysterious and terrifying, and it was natural to try to find a connection between the two.

HOUSECALL

When Goodwoman Phillips woke, it was light in the room and there was a visitor, a tall man in a long coat, unpacking a leather satchel and laying out items along the wooden bench under the window. A cup, a cloth, a knife. In a rush Goodwoman Phillips's dazed senses sharpened and she guessed who this man was, and why he was there.

"I'll not be bled." She tried for a firm, clear tone, but even to her own ears her voice was low and faltering. The doctor turned and looked at her calmly.

"Goody Phillips, your husband and sons have consulted me about your case. You have had fever now for several days. In such an instance, the recommended course of action is bleeding, to balance the humors within your body. I assure you it is for the best."

As the doctor spoke, he drew near. Goodwoman Phillips could see the knife glinting in his hand. Then it was done, a smooth, quick cut on her arm. Blood dripped into the cup he held up. Her head thudded and the room seemed to lift and tilt, then spin. Dizzy, she moaned and closed her eyes.

"Fainted," said the doctor. "Not uncommon for one so far gone with fever. We can but hope this bloodletting was done in time."

But Goodwoman Phillips didn't wake again. By midday, on Christmas Eve of 1664, she was dead.

IT'S NOT FUNNY, IT'S HUMORAL

From ancient times until the 19th century, when a doctor told you your humors were out of balance, he didn't mean that there was something wrong with your funny bone. Humoral theory was one of the key principles in Western medicine. According to this theory, first proposed by doctors in ancient Greece, the human body contained four humors, or fluids: black bile (also known as melancholy), yellow or red bile, blood, and phlegm. Everyone had a unique humoral makeup, or constitution, and your health depended on maintaining the right humoral balance, or mix of fluids, inside your body. Curing disease was a matter of putting the humors back in balance. This is where the idea of bleeding patients originated.

"GOD HAVE MERCY ON US!"

A neighbor woman came that afternoon to wash the body and prepare it for burial—although how exactly the body was to be buried, with the ground frozen hard, was a challenge the Phillips family had not yet considered. As it turned out, it was a problem they wouldn't have to solve. When the neighbor removed Goodwoman Phillips's nightdress, she gasped: large red rings had appeared on the dead woman's chest and back. Under her right arm was an ominous purple swelling.

"A buboe! Plague tokens!" whimpered the shaken woman. "Plain as my hand, these are the signs. This is a plague house. Oh, God have mercy on us!" She turned and fled from the house, racing to the parish office to raise the alarm.

Before long, there was a knocking at the door of the Phillipses' tiny house. The searcher had arrived. It was the searcher's duty to visit every house where a death occurred in St. Giles in the Fields, to examine the deceased and to report back to the parish clerk, who recorded the cause of death in the parish register.

All 119 London parishes kept registers of births and deaths, bulky volumes filled with line after line describing deaths from old age, from accidents, from illnesses of every kind. Yet of all the ways to die in 1664, none was more feared than plague, for plague was unstoppable—it could spread through a neighborhood like fire. In a matter of weeks, plague could engulf a whole city, even a whole country.

The searcher for St. Giles in the Field that day was a shrunken, wrinkled woman. She was desperately poor, and spent every cent she had on ale at the inn. It was well know that she'd gladly take a coin or two should a family wish to have the cause of death changed in the report she delivered to the parish clerk. For a small tip, a suicide could become an "accident." Even plague could be registered as a simple fever. But the Phillips family had no money to offer her. The sons had spent everything they had to bring the doctor in to bleed their mother.

The searcher peered down drunkenly at Goodwoman Phillips, then reeled away in alarm as she recognized the plague tokens. She staggered out of the house, muttering to herself, only to return soon afterward, bringing with her men from the parish office. Hurriedly, they removed Goodwoman Phillips's body. Then they began boarding up the doors and windows of the house, sealing the dead woman's husband and sons inside. Not until the parish was certain the house was free of plague would anyone be allowed to leave.

Inside the darkened house, Goodman Phillips and his sons listened as nail after nail was pounded into the boards blocking the windows. Finally, the pounding was replaced by the softer sound of brushes, and they knew that one of the men was painting a huge red cross on their door, and the words "God Have Mercy Upon Us," which announced to everyone in the neighborhood that this house was cursed with the plague.

That Christmas Eve, all was silent in the Phillips house. Goodwoman's husband and her sons knew that now they could only wait and wonder: Which of them would be next?

Outside, their neighbors crossed the street to avoid walking past the boarded-up house, fearing that if they came too close they would be contaminated with plague seeds. Overhead, the omen in the heavens appeared again, the fiery comet streaking across the black night sky. What did it mean? What new dreadful events could be coming?

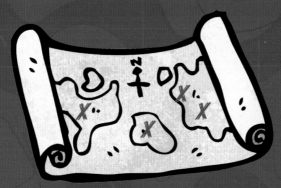

A TERRIFYING HISTORY

The first major epidemic of plague is believed to have been the Plague of Justinian. It began in the city of Constantinople in 541 CE, killing up to 60,000 people, then swept through Egypt and Persia over the next three years, bringing the death toll into the millions.

It wasn't until several hundred years later that plague reappeared, this time in Europe. Between 1347 and 1351, the Black Death decimated the population of medieval Europe, killing at least 25 million people. Some historians think that up to a third of the population of Europe died during this time.

There were profound economic and cultural changes across Europe as a result of the Black Death. People's religious faith was shaken by the suffering they witnessed, and their loyalty to the existing social order was weakened. So many peasants had died that large landowners had difficulty finding laborers to harvest their crops. For the first time, when peasants didn't like the wages being offered in their own community, they were likely to pick up and leave, traveling to the next town in search of better pay. Some historians trace the beginnings of capitalism to peasant revolts in the years following the Black Death. Gradually, the feudal system (in which peasants worked for their local landowner, or lord, in exchange for protection) collapsed, leading to the rise of the middle class.

Over the next 300 years, plague continued to revisit Europe sporadically, but it never killed again in the massive numbers seen during the years of the Black Death.

THE FEAR BUILDS

A little more than a week later, soon after New Year's, John Graunt stepped to the door of his London shop and tossed a coin to one of the ragged boys shivering in the frosty January air.

"Run to the coffeehouse on the corner, my lad, and fetch me a copy of the Bills of Mortality. The first bill of the year has been printed this very morning, and I'm devilish anxious to see it. You may find me in a generous mood to repay you for your speed." As he watched the boy disappear up the cobbled road, Graunt considered, not for the first time, how unlikely it was that the Bills of Mortality, a dry page of statistics compiled from the weekly reports of births and deaths in each of London's parishes, should have become so popular with readers all over the city. Each week in the coffeehouses and the taverns, conversation was sure to turn to the latest news in the bills—especially if there were unusual deaths to discuss.

John Graunt found the Bills of Mortality fascinating reading at any time, but he'd heard that in this week's bill there was something he would find particularly interesting. And when the errand boy returned, panting, with the page fluttering in his hands, it didn't take long for Graunt to spot it: "Death by Plague — 1."

In the mid-17th century, an occasional death from plague was not uncommon, and though it created anxiety in the immediate neighborhood, it generally didn't mean that an epidemic was about to occur. In fact, London hadn't had an epidemic of plague for nearly 20 years. And plague, as John Graunt and everyone else knew, was most to be feared in the hot months of summer, not in the midst of the coldest winter that anyone could remember. But all the same, John Graunt decided it would be wise to keep a close eye on the bills over the next few months.

Throughout the rest of that cold, dark winter, while all of London was watching the sky, John Graunt was scanning the lists of deaths in the city, reading the signs there that told him an epidemic of plague was coming again.

LOOKING FOR ANSWERS

hat did John Graunt know that no one else in London did? Quite a bit, actually. Graunt was the owner of a popular drapers and haberdashery business. His shop sold cloth, from the coarsest cottons to the finest silks and velvets, as well as buttons, thread, and ribbons in every color of the rainbow.

But running a successful business wasn't enough to keep Graunt's active mind occupied. He longed to be a scientist or a scholar. During the long evenings, with the shop closed and his family asleep, he had found himself casting about for a subject of study, something through which he could make a name for himself. He'd always been fascinated with the Bills of Mortality, and he had saved several years' worth of the weekly statistics. In the late 1650s, Graunt had started to realize just how useful the information in those dusty stacks of printed sheets could be.

As a businessman, he knew the value of having information about his customers. He needed to know approximately how many births to expect each year, so that he could stock the right amount of delicate linen for christening robes. And by knowing how many deaths there might be in a year, he could have enough cloth for mourning clothes on hand. At the time, there was no source for this kind of data. Graunt, like other shopkeepers, was forced to depend on his intuition and experience when ordering his stock. Yet the weekly Bills of Mortality, which had been printed since an earlier plague year, 1592, contained this information. If someone was determined enough to read through each bill, Graunt figured, adding up the deaths and the births, he would no doubt see averages emerge, and find useful patterns. With that realization, Graunt had begun to wonder how many other uses there might be for information about rates of births and deaths in his city. Comparing the numbers of deaths and the causes from one year to another might reveal patterns in not only how many people were dying, but also why.

He decided that he had found his subject.

VARIETY IS THE SPICE OF DEATH

There were many ways to die in London in 1665 besides plague. The Bills of Mortality listed, among other unfamiliar causes of death: flux (diarrhea), imposthume (an abscess or boil), overlaid (obesity), rising of the lights (hysteria), and tissick (asthma). In addition, there were records in the bills for deaths occurring as a result of "Horseshoehead," "Stoppage in the Stomach," "Twisting of the Guts," and "Eaten by Lice."

SUCCESS AT LAST

Graunt collected all of the bills published over the past 60 years and studied them closely, looking for the secrets that they held about London life. In 1662 he published a slim volume loftily titled *Natural and political observations, mentioned in a following Index, and made upon the Bills of Mortality: With reference to the Government, Religion, Trade, Growth, Air, Diseases and the several changes of the said City.*

His book was an instant hit, and it gave John Graunt the recognition he craved. In 1663 Graunt was admitted to a very exclusive club of scientists: the Royal Society of London for Improving Natural Knowledge.

Although Graunt modestly described his accomplishment as just "shopkeeper's mathematics," the king himself had recommended that Graunt be made a member of the Royal Society. It could be that King Charles II was grateful. Graunt's calculations made it clear that one of the more persistent rumors about plague—that an epidemic of the disease followed every coronation—was false. That didn't stop most people from believing it, but it helped the king to have science on his side.

But Graunt's biggest discovery? He had found a way to predict the arrival of a plague year. This was an earth-shaking scientific advance. For more than a century, London had been ravaged by regular epidemics of plague, one approximately every 20 years. Tens of thousands had died, and the city's population lived in fear of the next outbreak.

By studying the Bills of Mortality, Graunt had

learned that in the months leading up to an outbreak of plague, the death rates from all causes were significantly higher than usual. "Sickly years," he called them. And in the winter of 1664, he could see from the weekly Bills of Mortality that London was in the midst of a very sickly year. Goodwoman Phillips's death, the first one to be recorded as plague, was not going to be last, of that he felt certain.

But why exactly would deaths from other causes increase in the months before the plague struck? Graunt thought he had an answer to that, too.

TOOLS OF THE TRADE

DESCRIPTIVE EPIDEMIOLOGY

Epidemiology depends on being able to look at the big picture of disease outbreak. Instead of helping individual patients get well—the physician's job—epidemiologists try to understand who is getting sick and why, how the disease is spreading, and how it can be stopped.

Today, most countries have sophisticated systems for tracking deaths and reports of unusual or infectious diseases, but in 1665 there was very little information of this kind. John Graunt was the first person in England to realize how important statistics could be for fighting disease on a city-wide or national scale.

Graunt's analysis of the Bills of Mortality for 1665 is one of the earliest examples of "descriptive epidemiology": the first step in the investigation of a disease outbreak. To get the big-picture views, scientists collect data that allows them to describe the situation: the who, where, and when of the outbreak. The answers to these questions often provide clues to how and why the epidemic is spreading—information that scientists can use to fight the disease.

GRAUNT'S THEORY IS PROVEN

John Graunt's ability to predict the coming of the plague was based on his intimate knowledge of the system for collecting death statistics in London. There were no coroners (professionals who investigate the causes of deaths) at the time, and frequently, especially among the poor, there was no doctor in attendance at a deathbed to fill out an official death certificate. In 1603, King James I had ordered the Worshipful Company of Parish Clerks to record and report births and deaths, including their causes, for each parish—the district surrounding a church— in and around London. But how could a few dozen parish clerks monitor all the births and deaths that occurred each week in the teeming streets of London? The king left that to the clerks to figure out.

In the end, they did it by employing searchers like the one who had visited Goodwoman Phillips's home.

As John Graunt saw it, there were two major weaknesses with this system. The first was that the searchers rarely had any medical background. So, while they were able to determine the cause of death fairly accurately in some cases (for instance, if there had been a drowning or a murder), much of the time they were only guessing. This led to some interesting causes of death appearing in the Bills of Mortality, including "teeth," "pining," "evil," "fools etc.," and the plain and simple "found dead."

The other weak point in the system was that the only people willing to take on the hazardous and despised duties of a searcher were poor, and they were badly paid for their services.

GRAUNT'S LEGACY

John Graunt's discovery that plague years were preceded by "sickly years" was a huge step forward in our understanding of how to accurately track diseases. His recommendation— that doctors and health officials pay close attention to all unexplained increases in death rates—has been helping epidemiologists understand, track, and stop disease outbreaks ever since. Or at least most of the time. Sometimes, Graunt's advice has been hard to follow, or forgotten.

For instance, it was only *after* the Spanish influenza pandemic in the early 20th century that investigator Wade Hampton Frost realized reported rates of pneumonia had been unusually high in the months leading up to the massive outbreak of the flu in U.S. army camps. With hindsight, Frost considered it very likely that what doctors had been calling pneumonia had actually been early cases of Spanish influenza. If someone had remembered John Graunt's lesson, Spanish influenza might have been stopped earlier. Had doctors been able to investigate the reasons for the sudden rise in the numbers of pneumonia patients, it might have led to an earlier identification of the illness. The Spanish flu swept through military camps across the United States before going global and killing millions worldwide in the winter of 1918.

This meant you could bribe them easily. When the real cause of death was plague, there was considerable urgency in bribing the searcher to cover it up. Otherwise, the family of the dead person knew they were doomed to be shut up in the house, with a vastly increased risk of coming down with plague themselves. For the price of a drink and a few extra pennies, many searchers would agree to write down whatever cause of death was suggested to them.

Graunt estimated that up to 20 percent of plague deaths were "mistakenly" recorded under other causes of death. That meant the epidemics that periodically engulfed London actually had much longer lead times than it would appear from a casual reading of the Bills of Mortality. He also noted that the parish clerks, because they were officials of the Anglican Church, recorded only the births and deaths of citizens who were also church members. In 1665, this was nearly everybody, but there were significant numbers of people in London who belonged to other religious groups: Jews, Catholics, Quakers, and Non-Conformists. Leaving out these groups meant that there were big gaps in the collected statistics.

There were a few more scattered plague deaths in London through the rest of that cold winter and spring. As the weather turned balmy, the numbers began to increase. In the first week of June, 43 deaths from plague were recorded—as many as there had been for the whole year up till then. The next week, there were 112.

Soon, anyone who could afford to leave the city began packing their bags. Husbands who stayed to mind their businesses sent their wives and children to the country. The king and all the members of his court left. Parliament was cancelled. Yet John Graunt stayed where he was. He had his shop to look after, but more importantly, he wanted to monitor the information that was coming in from the various parishes each week. His theory about sickly years leading to plague years was being proven before his very eyes.

"HOW EMPTY THE STREETS ARE"

By mid-July, there were over a thousand plague deaths a week in London. By September that had increased to more than a thousand a day. In late August a Londoner named Samuel Pepys had written in his diary, "But now, how few people I see, and those walking like people that have taken leave of the world." The city, deserted by almost all who could flee, had taken on an eerie silence.

Pepys was a successful businessman, a supplier to the Royal Navy. But unlike most wealthy people, he didn't leave London during the plague. Instead, he stayed and recorded his impressions in his diary, which was published almost two centuries later. It is still one of the most revealing records about what life was like for people in London during that terrible year.

In the fall, with plague raging across the city, Pepys noted, "Lord, how empty the streets are, and melancholy, so many poor sick people in the streets, full of sores, and so many sad stories overheard as I walk, everybody talking of this dead, and that man sick, and so many in this place, and so many in that. And they tell me that in Westminster there is never a physitian, and but one apothecary left, all being dead—but that there are great hopes of a great decrease this week. God send it." Slowly, the numbers of plague deaths did begin to decrease, as fall turned to winter and the weather became colder.

At the end of the year, as people began to cautiously return to the city, John Graunt published a booklet entitled *London's dreadful visitation, or, A collection of all the Bills of Mortality for this present year*, which analyzed the consequences of the terrible epidemic. By December, more than 68,000 plague deaths had been recorded in a population previously estimated at 450,000. Fifteen percent of the people of London had died of plague.

THE COTTON CONNECTION

No one knows exactly how or why the Great Plague of 1665 started. But one theory is that infected rats and fleas may have traveled to London along with bales of cotton from Holland. Just the year before, in 1663–64, more than 50,000 people had died in a devastating plague epidemic in Amsterdam.

The location of the first deaths in the London epidemic support this theory. St. Giles in the Fields was a parish where many dock workers lived—the people who would have unloaded the boats and transported the cotton bales into the heart of London for sale. These workers could have been bitten by plague-infected fleas. The irony? John Graunt, a wealthy draper and haber-dasher, may have been selling cloth made from that very cotton in his shop, while spending his evenings tracking the spread of the epidemic through his city.

NEW KNOWLEDGE, BUT NO CURE

For the first time, by looking carefully at statistics, someone had partially solved the mysteries surrounding plague. Hundreds of years later, scientists would remember what John Graunt had accomplished.

Yet even with Graunt's discoveries, much about plague remained a puzzle in 1665. How did the disease start? And how did it spread? Did you catch it from breathing infected air? From contact with a victim? Or did you get it from something you ate or drank? Most terrifyingly of all, was it simply God's will that the people of London should suffer?

Because medical knowledge was quite basic at the time, nearly every theory was taken seriously. There was immense variety in the proposed methods of preventing plague. Some doctors held gold coins in their mouths while they treated patients, believing that the metal gave them protection. Others recommended that herbs and spices combined with vinegar or tar be burned to cleanse the air of sickrooms. Many people chewed or smoked tobacco, in the belief that it purified the air. Schoolboys at Eton, an exclusive private school, were punished if they forgot to smoke each morning before their prayers. Other people wore protective amulets, some containing toad poison. Con artists sold all kinds of exotic wonder drugs to the gullible and the desperate, including powdered unicorn horn, phoenix eggs, and the kidney stones of camels.

UNEQUAL TREATMENT

Although wealthy and middle-class plague patients during the 17th century could afford doctors, there weren't many options for the thousands of poor people who succumbed to plague.

A few books and pamphlets of the time suggested low-cost treatments or offered recipes for "cures" that could be made at home. In 1665, the Royal College of Physicians published *Certain Necessary Directions for the Prevention and Cure of the Plague*, which recommended a sure-fire method for reducing swelling in the enlarged lymph glands—a symptom that tormented plague sufferers: "Do not leave the poorer sort destitute of good remedies: Pull off the feathers from the tails of living cocks, hens, pigeons, or chickens, and holding their bills, hold them hard to the Botch or Swelling and so keep them at that part until they [the birds] die; and by this means draw out the poison."

No chickens handy? There were alternatives: "Take a great onion, hollow it, put into it a fig cut small... put it into a wet paper, and roast it in embers; apply it hot unto the tumour."

For the wealthy, the most highly regarded "cure" was the legendary Venice Treacle, which required nearly 60 ingredients, some commonplace (such as cinnamon, pepper, honey, and cloves) and others much more exotic (viper flesh, opium, beaver glands, and Dead Sea salts). London Treacle was also popular—a mixture of cumin seeds, bayberries, snake root, cloves, and honey, it was less costly and easier to obtain or to make.

But there were far fewer ways to treat plague than there were so-called preventatives. Although patients frequently died from loss of blood after being bled, doctors continued to use this method of treatment. Sweating was less deadly but still unpleasant. It was based on the idea that since plague caused fevers, it should be treated with heat. The sweat the sufferer produced was thought to cleanse the body of plague poisons. If all else failed, there was opium, which at least dulled the pain for the plague victim. When that too failed, there was only prayer.

Meanwhile, until the Great Plague of 1665 subsided in early 1666, wagons continued to rattle slowly up and down the nearly deserted cobbled streets of London, collecting the dead.

John Graunt's grim totaling of the numbers showed that there had been only 9,967 christenings, compared to 97,306 burials, in all of London that year. Could the city recover from such a blow?

Graunt was confident it could. London was an incredibly dangerous place to live at all times, he pointed out. There were far more deaths in the city each year than there were births, and yet the city continued to grow. People from the surrounding countryside were constantly coming to London, looking for work and a better life, and Graunt predicted that within a few years the population of London would rebound. Again, he was right. Slowly, life began to return to normal in the city, as people forgot the year of terror and death.

FLEAS AND RATS AND PLAGUE, OH NO!

We now know the path plague takes to get to humans. *Yersinia pestis* bacteria is constantly present at low levels in populations of certain rodents, who form what scientists call "the reservoir" for the bacteria.

Rodents who may carry *Yersinia pestis* include squirrels, prairie dogs, chipmunks, rabbits, mice, voles, and rats. Rats have proven to be the big problem for humans, one type in particular. The *Rattus norvegicus*, or Norwegian rat, showed up in Europe around 1000 CE, and it quickly decided that human habitats— towns and cities—were ideal sources for food and shelter.

As they spread throughout Europe, Norwegian rats brought along some annoying roommates: the *Yersinia pestis* bacteria in their guts and bloodstream, and the fleas that lived in their fur and feasted on their blood. Those fleas weren't too fussy about where they got their meals, either. They would happily bite a human, when one was available. And in the crowded, unsanitary living conditions of European towns and cities in the Middle Ages, humans were very often available. For some unlucky people, those itchy flea bites weren't just an annoyance—they were deadly.

FINDING ANSWERS IN HONG KONG

I t would be nearly 230 years before anyone solved the mystery of the source of plague, and it would happen in the midst of another terrible epidemic, in another part of the world entirely. In January 1894, an epidemic of bubonic plague broke out in Hong Kong, and by the following June it had caused over 80,000 deaths, mostly among poor Chinese laborers in the city. The governor of Hong Kong, Sir William Robinson, issued an international call for scientists to travel to the afflicted city to search for solutions. He was delighted when an eminent Japanese scientist, Shibasaburo Kitasato, answered his plea for help.

Scientists and doctors in Hong Kong gave Kitasato his own laboratory and a full staff of assistants. In fact, there was so much excitement about Kitasato's arrival that everyone overlooked

another researcher who had also arrived
in Hong Kong. Alexander Yersin was a
Swiss bacteriologist who had been
practicing medicine in the French
colony of Indochina (now the countries
of Vietnam and Cambodia). Unlike Kitasato,
Yersin was given neither a warm welcome nor a
laboratory space. He had to pay to have his own lab built,
a lowly straw hut located alongside the much grander building
occupied by Kitasato's offices.

Despite the fact that Kitasato was so much better supplied
than Yersin, the two scientists quickly got caught up in a race,
each trying to be the first to discover the source of plague. Their
competition was so fierce that Kitasato tried to prevent Yersin
from getting access to the bodies of plague victims. Yersin was
forced to bribe the soldiers guarding the plague wards of hospitals
in order to get the blood and tissue samples he needed.

That June, each man announced that he had successfully
isolated the bacteria that causes plague. Kitasato was initially
credited with the discovery, but eventually the scientific
community decided that Yersin had been the first, and the
bacteria was named *Yersinia pestis* in his honor. Yersin also
developed the first plague vaccine, which was used with limited
success during an outbreak of plague in Bombay (now Mumbai),
India, in 1896. In addition, he was the first to suspect that rats
played a role in the transmission of bubonic plague, although
that discovery was eventually made by a French researcher,
Paul-Louis Simmond, in 1897.

Simmond's research showed that fleas called *Xenopsylla
cheopis* were the agents transferring the infection from rat to rat;
when the rats died, the fleas passed the disease to humans.
It took nearly 40 years for Simmond's research to be accepted by
the scientific and medical community, but the mystery of plague
was finally solved.

THREE PLAGUES, ONE CAUSE

There are three types of plague: bubonic, pneumonic, and septicemic. All three forms are caused by the same bacteria, *Yersinia pestis*.

Bubonic plague is the most famous and the most feared, but it is actually the least deadly of the three. In bubonic plague, the bacteria attacks the lymphatic system, causing lymph nodes in the patient's neck, underarms, or groin to develop painful swellings (traditionally called buboes), as well as reddish or purple markings on the skin. In 17th-century England, these round marks were known as plague tokens. Before the buboes or plague tokens appear, the patient suffers fever, headaches, chills, vomiting, and extreme exhaustion. Historically, more than half of all bubonic plague sufferers died, usually within two weeks of the appearance of buboes.

Pneumonic plague, which attacks the lungs and is spread through the air by coughing and sneezing, is even more deadly, killing nearly everyone who contracts the illness. Victims, who generally die within two to four days, suffer fever and headache at first, then begin coughing up blood. Soon, their lungs fill with fluid and they can no longer breathe.

In septicemic plague, the rarest form of the disease, the bacteria infects the patient's bloodstream. Death can occur so quickly that sometimes no symptoms appear. When there are symptoms, they include fever and weakness, followed by bleeding from the mouth and nose, and internal bleeding. Generally, without treatment, this form of plague kills victims in less than a day.

Today, antibiotics can successfully treat about 85 percent of plague cases—but only if the drugs are started during the first 24 hours after infection.

PLAGUE IN MODERN TIMES

Today, plague can be successfully treated with antibiotics if patients get medical attention in time. But the disease is still a feared killer. In 1993, south and central India were rattled by a severe earthquake that damaged a number of cities, including Bangalore, Bombay, Hyderabad, and Madras, as well as many smaller villages and towns. In the earthquake's aftermath, huge shantytowns and slums sprang up to house people who had been left homeless by the disaster. The shantytowns also sheltered large numbers of rats.

In September 1994, plague broke out in one of the largest slums, in the city of Surat. Fifty-five people died—an insignificant number compared to the terrible death tolls of the medieval plague epidemics, but enough to cause panic around the world. Commercial air traffic to and from India stopped, the stock market in India crashed, trade halted, and the media went crazy speculating about the possibility that plague could spread to other countries, triggering a massive pandemic (global epidemic). Luckily, it didn't happen.

Since the Indian epidemic, there have been outbreaks of plague in Algeria and other parts of Africa. Each time, international medical teams from the World Health Organization and the Centers for Disease Control have been able to contain the outbreaks. But the WHO lists plague as a "re-emerging disease"— a possible threat that requires constant monitoring and vigilance.

PLOTTING A MYSTERY

THE SOHO CHOLERA OUTBREAK OF 1854

Srah, wake up. The baby's crying."

Sarah Lewis groaned and rolled over, trying to ignore her husband's whispers. It felt as if she'd only just closed her eyes. How could the baby be awake already?

She opened one eye to squint at the light streaming in through her thin curtains. Here in London's crowded Soho district, in the heart of the world's biggest city, the noise never went away entirely at night, but it did quiet down. Now the noise was building again, as the 2 million residents of London began their day. Sarah could hear the clatter of horses' hooves, the trundle of wagons and carriages rolling over cobbled streets, the hoarse shouts of vendors and beggars and newspaper boys. Cutting through it all was the earsplitting jangle of a hopeful early-morning organ grinder.

Sarah yawned. It sounded like morning had come to Broad Street. But what had Thomas meant about the baby crying? Their daughter, just six months old, was fretful and sickly, and they were used to waking up to her wails. But there were no cries this morning that Sarah could hear.

She lay still and concentrated. There was the deep, regular breathing of her husband lying beside her, and the lighter breaths of her two children, sleeping on their pallets on the floor alongside the bed. And yes, there was a tiny whimpering, barely audible, coming from the baby's cradle.

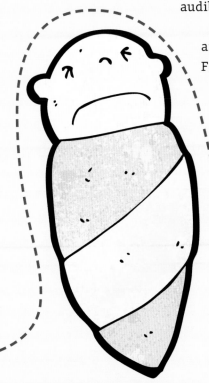

Throwing back the sheets, Sarah rose and crossed the room to check on little Frances. She bent over the cradle, crooning a soft morning greeting, but the smile on her face quickly changed to wide-eyed alarm.

Frances was thrashing in pain. Her small, pale face glistened with sweat, and her clothes and bedding were soaked with watery diarrhea. Sarah snatched up her baby and rushed to her husband. "Thomas, run for the doctor," she implored. "Right away!"

NOTHING TO FRET ABOUT

Dr. Rogers, when he arrived later that morning, calmed Sarah's fears. The baby was simply suffering from summer diarrhea, he explained, a not uncommon complaint among young children in hot weather. However, Frances would need careful nursing to bring her back to health. He advised Sarah of various remedies: a small spoonful of castor oil or syrup of rhubarb would help to expel the harmful illness, and a teaspoonful of brandy, mixed with hot water and given every hour, would calm the baby's stomach. To ease the cramps that had her daughter curled in pain, Sarah could apply a mustard plaster, made by mixing flour, water, and mustard powder, to the baby's tummy. If that didn't work, she could send to the local chemist's shop for laudanum. A few drops diluted in water would soon quiet little Frances.

"Terrible smell in the streets today, isn't there?" the doctor said as he packed up his medical bag. "Not surprising that the child's ill, really, with such foul air about. Is there a cesspool near?"

Taking him to the front window, Sarah pointed out the opening to the house's cesspool, just beside the front step, and directly under the Lewis family's windows. "The smell is dreadful in this warm weather, but the cesspool's so handy for throwing out the slops. And 40 Broad Street's the best house on the street for a young family: we've got the water pump just beside us, so we can fill the water bucket on the same trip," she explained.

That afternoon, Sarah did just that. While baby Frances tossed in an uneasy doze in her cradle, her mother wrung out the dirty sheets, which had been soaking all morning in buckets of water. A full bucket in each hand, Sarah made her way carefully out the front door and down the steps, tipping the contents— the disgusting greenish soup of diarrhea and water made her stomach turn—into the cesspool. Then she continued over a few paces to join the lineup at the Broad Street water pump, refilling her buckets with wash water after a short wait.

THE ANGEL OF DEATH VISITS

But Frances's summer diarrhea kept getting worse instead of better. Just a day later, Frances was so weak she couldn't even whimper. Her eyes were sunk into her head, and to her mother's distress, her skin took on a blue-ish tinge. Sarah fought back her worry and set herself to the task of nursing: gently rocking the cradle, quietly singing, stroking Frances's back, trying to tempt her to eat. She only left the family's small room to empty the slop pail or to fetch more water.

Usually Sarah loved the chatter and gossip in the lineup at the pump. Now, with all her energies concentrated on the small, fragile life at home, she didn't linger to listen to the latest neighborhood news. Even so, she was aware that all was not right on Broad Street—a strange silence had come over the place.

Where was the clatter and turmoil, the nonstop rumble of wagons, the shouts of the street sellers? Even the organ grinders had deserted Broad Street, it seemed. The only sounds Sarah now heard from outside in the wee hours of the night were occasional running footsteps or muffled cries. That night there was the sound of someone sobbing.

Sarah's husband, Thomas, a police constable, knew only too well what was wrong, but he was reluctant to further worry his preoccupied young wife. Finally, on the third evening of baby Frances's illness, he arrived home and sat down heavily at the table. "Sarah," he said flatly, "there's sickness and death all through Soho. I've seen the hearse outside almost every house up and down Broad Street. They say today there are so many dead, they're piling them two and three deep in the undertaker's wagon. It's cholera, so they say. Everyone who can is leaving. We've got to go too. Perhaps my brother in the country will take us in."

He handed his wife a newspaper. "Look here. It's even in the papers."

Reluctantly, Sarah read the article he pointed out: "...this district was attacked by a pestilence which has unfortunately swept away a large number of persons who were, the day before, in perfect health. On Friday morning people might be seen before break of day running in all directions for medical advice. The angel of death had spread his wings over the place... it becomes the duty of all who have an interest in the welfare of the community to investigate the causes of this sudden and frightful attack."

Her face grim, Sarah handed the paper back to Thomas. "We'll keep the windows shut tight against the sickness. We won't go out unless we must. But to move that child now would be the death of her."

Sarah's voice was defiant, but she was fighting back tears. Like everyone in London, she knew that cholera was almost always fatal. The doctors suspected it came from poisoned air rising from garbage heaps, the polluted river, and the raw sewage running in the city's gutters. With the heavy summer heat hanging over London, the stink of rot and sewage was growing worse each day. But until Frances had recovered from this bout of summer diarrhea, they had to stay put and hope for the best.

CURES FOR A PENNY

While doctors and scientists debated the causes of cholera, quacks and snake-oil salesmen competed to develop and market miraculous cure-all potions. Newspapers of the day were filled with advertisements for dubious cholera treatments. A typical ad would read like this one, for a cure-all sold in the fancy shops of Regent Circus: "FEVER and CHOLERA— The air of every sick room should be purified by using SAUNDER'S ANTI-MEPHITIC FLUID. This powerful disinfectant destroys foul smells in a moment, and impregnates the air with a refreshing fragrance."

While it seems laughable today that anyone would believe a perfume could cure cholera, in the 19th century people were desperate, ready to try anything. Some of the recommended medical treatments were downright dangerous! Doctors commonly fought cholera with laudanum (a drug extracted from opium, similar to today's morphine), calomel (mercury), and camphor. Laudanum relieved pain, but it was highly addictive, and children or adults could easily overdose on it. Calomel is now known to be very toxic, and even in small doses it induces vomiting and diarrhea. Camphor, which was used as a disinfectant, is a strong-smelling substance from the wood of the camphor laurel tree, and it is poisonous too.

Some doctors believed purging would get rid of the poisons, so they often prescribed castor oil, a powerful laxative. In a public notice from 1831, the City of London Board of Health recommended swallowing a spoonful of mustard mixed in half a pint of warm water, to induce vomiting. Treatments like these must have dramatically increased the death count in cholera epidemics.

The irony is that the cure for cholera couldn't be simpler: clean water. Lots and lots of it. Cholera causes massive fluid loss from vomiting and diarrhea, but if patients can stay hydrated, they nearly always survive. Today, cholera patients take oral rehydration salts or receive fluids intravenously. If properly treated, less than 1 percent of people who contract the disease will die.

IT'S ALL GONE QUIET

Sadly, the next day—September 2—Dr. Rogers was called upon to make a return trip to the Lewis family's room. Baby Frances, after four long days of struggle, had died. Dr. Rogers noted on the death certificate that the cause of death was "exhaustion, after an attack of diarrhea four days previous."

By now Broad Street was almost deserted. There was no one lined up at the pump, the shops were closed, the curtains drawn in the windows up and down the length of the block. It was an uncanny stillness in the midst of one of the most densely populated areas on the planet. Along the two short blocks of Broad Street stood 49 houses—formerly grand houses of the aristocracy, now mostly rented out to poor laborers—that offered shelter to an astounding 860 people. Almost every room housed an entire family, who did their cooking, washing, sleeping, and living within its crowded space. Squeezed in behind the houses and along the alleys were cowsheds, slaughterhouses, and breweries, even a factory for making bullets. All had now gone quiet.

On September 3, the evening silence on Broad Street was broken by a distant set of footsteps, coming closer. A man appeared. He headed straight for the street's water pump. From a leather case he took out a small glass bottle, which he filled with water. He capped it, put it to his eye and stared at the clear liquid for a moment or two, then put the bottle back into the case and strapped it closed. From the clinking as he walked off, it seemed that there might be other bottles inside as well.

This unusual man was a doctor and a scientist, and at a time when most people broke down in panic at the words "cholera epidemic," to him the Broad Street outbreak was a golden opportunity. He was John Snow—a man who thought he had solved the mystery of cholera, and who was looking for a way to prove it.

KNOW YOUR ENEMY

D r. John Snow had been fighting cholera for more than 20 years. When he was just 19 years old and the new apprentice to a surgeon in the north of England, Snow was sent to the mining town of Killingworth, where the first of the great cholera epidemics of the 19th century was devastating the population. There, he struggled for weeks to help the sick and dying, seeing firsthand the terrible conditions in which the miners were forced to work.

In a letter to his family, he observed, "The pit is one huge privy, and of course the men always take their victuals with unwashed hands." Today we realize that unhygienic conditions are a perfect breeding ground for disease, but at the time Snow's observations were unorthodox.

The medical thinking of the day held that cholera and other diseases were the result of "miasma," a fog of infected air rising from piles of garbage and sewage. But Snow knew cholera caused severe diarrhea, which led him to question whether bad air was the real culprit. Since the disease clearly affected the digestive system, wasn't it reasonable to assume that the "poison" causing cholera was something that you ingested—something in food or water?

THE GREAT DEBATE: MIASMA OR GERMS?

Today it seems odd that so many people, including most doctors, believed disease floated around in invisible clouds called miasma. How did this idea get started, and why did people believe in it for so long?

The term "miasma" comes from the ancient Greek word for pollution, and its use dates back to the third century BCE. Hippocrates, a Greek doctor who is often called the first epidemiologist, described the theory of miasma in his writings, which doctors throughout Europe studied for hundreds of years. Miasma was thought to be a poisonous mist or vapor, rising up from rotting garbage and organic matter. We can see just how well-accepted the idea was by looking at the names of some diseases. Malaria, for instance, comes from the Italian *mal aria*: literally, "bad air." By the 19th century nearly everyone equated bad smells with disease.

Even after scientists like John Snow—and later Robert Koch, who in the 1880s was the first to identify the bacteria that causes cholera—proved that germs, not miasma, were the sources of disease, many people refused to change their opinions. Florence Nightingale, the founder of modern nursing, believed until the day she died in 1910 that miasma was the source of many diseases, and she championed cleanliness, hygiene, fresh air, and sunshine as ways to prevent and cure disease. Nightingale's emphasis on the importance of high standards of hygiene in hospitals has saved millions of lives, and she was right that there is a connection between poor sanitation and diseases such as cholera and typhoid. But the connection is germs, not smells.

And since the mines were both unhygienic and crowded, wasn't it also reasonable to think that the men might be passing cholera from one to another, perhaps through traces of infected feces that they were accidentally ingesting?

Snow kept his suspicions to himself—after all, at this point he hadn't even been to medical school yet. He knew his ideas would be laughed at. But he didn't forget about them—he waited for an opportunity to prove his theory. In the meantime, he kept busy.

By the 1840s, Dr. John Snow had a thriving medical practice as one of the world's first anesthesiologists (pronounced an-es-thee-zee-awl-o-jists), administering the newly discovered "sleeping gases" (chloroform and ether) to patients about to undergo surgery. This innovation was a huge breakthrough for surgeons (and patients!). Before the discovery of ether, surgeons had operated on people who were fully awake. There are stories of bleeding patients sprinting out of the room and hiding in closets to escape from surgeons and the terrible pain they inflicted.

John Snow had immediately seen the advantages of ether and chloroform, and he invented a regulator to deliver a safe, steady flow of gas to patients. He quickly became so famous, and so respected for his skill, that he was asked to give chloroform to Queen Victoria during the births of two of her children.

Snow's growing knowledge about the properties of gases made him even more convinced that miasma couldn't be the cause of cholera. He'd learned how concentrated the doses of chloroform and ether had to be in order to put patients to sleep even briefly, so it didn't make sense that clouds of bad air could infect people throughout an entire city. And if bad air was really causing cholera, why didn't everyone develop the disease? The theory of miasma seemed full of logical inconsistencies, but he had no way to test his suspicions.

Then cholera came back. A new epidemic of the disease was sweeping Europe, and in the spring of 1853, a year before the Broad Street outbreak, the disease hit South London, the part of the city that lay along the south bank of the River Thames.

As with earlier outbreaks, no one understood how or why cholera was spreading. Theories abounded. Some speculated that the people in the poor neighborhoods along the river were "morally susceptible"—that defects in their character made them prone to developing cholera. The miasmatists insisted that the smell from the neighborhoods and the river caused the disease to run rampant. Others argued it was a combination of the two factors.

But John Snow started wondering where the people along the river got their drinking water.

THE GRAND EXPERIMENT

There was only one way to find out—by asking. So every evening, all summer long, John Snow went from house to house in South London, knocking on doors, inquiring how many people in each home had gotten sick and how many had died. Then he would follow up with an unexpected question: "Do you know which company supplies your water?"

In the neighborhoods south of the river, most people no longer got their water from public pumps, but had it piped in from the River Thames. There were two private water companies supplying that part of London: Lambeth and Southwark & Vauxhall. While Lambeth piped in water from a relatively clean part of the river upstream, Southwark & Vauxhall drew their water downstream from the main sewer lines, which poured the city's waste into the water. Would that difference affect who got sick? Snow suspected it would.

Significantly, there was no predictable pattern to the water supply system: one house might be supplied by Lambeth, while all its nearest neighbors got water from Southwark & Vauxhall. If Snow could show cholera struck only the homes supplied with dirty water, it would be strong proof that miasma was not the cause. He hoped that his "Grand Experiment" would establish once and for all that cholera was spread through contaminated water.

Before Snow could complete his investigations, however, the Broad Street outbreak began. This terrible epidemic was confined to a very small area, he realized. Could he apply the techniques he had been using in South London, find the source of the outbreak, and do it fast enough to halt the epidemic, or to stop it from spreading beyond Soho? He knew he had to try.

THE SEARCH BROADENS

now marched up and down the streets of Soho, taking samples from all the local pumps. He hoped he'd be able to identify some contaminant. But when he got the vials of water home, they all seemed to be clear.

Snow wasn't a man to be easily discouraged. He took to the streets again, knocking on doors, asking the same odd questions: "Has anyone in this house had cholera? Where do you get your water?"

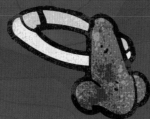

DO YOU SMELL
WHAT I SMELL?

In 1854, London—with its 2.5 million people—was the biggest city to date in the history of humankind. And it was unquestionably the greatest city of the age, with grand palaces, crowded playhouses, and Europe's foremost parliament. But it didn't have a city-wide sewer system, a dump, or even a garbage collector. The result? London was drowning in its own filth.

Many houses, particularly older homes in poor areas, had no running water and weren't connected to a sewer. Instead, each house had its own cesspool, a large underground pit where waste was deposited. When the pit filled up, the landlord called in the "night-soil men," who hauled the contents away in a wagon to farms on the edge of town. This system worked well for a long time, but London was growing fast and the edge of town was getting further and further away. The night-soil men raised their prices, and soon landlords were putting off having their cesspools emptied. The cesspools frequently overflowed, flooding cellars with human waste.

The situation wasn't much better even if you lived in a house that was connected to a sewer. Where did the sewers empty? Into the Thames, the river that flowed through the heart of London. And from where did London's water supply come? The Thames!

Using the river as both a sewer and a water source created a perfect environment for spreading disease. All that sewage also made the city incredibly smelly. And human waste wasn't the only problem. London was full of industry and animals. All of these sources contributed waste and garbage and their own particular smells. So it's not too surprising that people connected the epidemics that periodically raged across the city with London's most immediately identifiable problem: its stink.

Over and over, he heard the same answer: "The Broad Street pump."

Very soon, he had made some startling discoveries. While Broad Street and the streets and alleys immediately surrounding it were the hardest hit by cholera, there were some unexplained exceptions. For instance, just around the corner, at 50 Poland Street, there had been only two deaths reported—and 50 Poland Street was the address of the St. James Workhouse, a charity home where more than 500 of Soho's poorest men, women, and children were housed and fed. Why had the cholera hardly touched these residents, while killing so many of their neighbors? The only difference he could find between the workhouse and the houses to either side was that the workhouse had its own well, right on the premises.

There was one other location in the neighborhood that seemed to have been passed over by the epidemic: the brewery on Broad Street. When John Snow asked the brewery owner for information about where the workers got their water, the surprising answer was that they didn't drink water. They were given a ration of beer every day, and drank that instead.

In just a few days, Snow was convinced that the evidence pointed to the Broad Street pump as the source of the outbreak. But there was one death he couldn't account for. Susannah Eley, an elderly lady living in Hampstead Heath, a wealthy area across town, had died of cholera on September 2. The date put her right in the midst of the Broad Street outbreak, yet what could her connection to the Soho epidemic be?

With a few more questions up and down Broad Street, Snow got his answer.

Susannah's sons operated the Eley Percussion Cap factory on Broad Street, and every day they had a jug of cold water, fresh from the Broad Street pump, transported across the city for their mother, who thought it the best-tasting water in all of London. Susannah Eley's love for the water from the Broad Street pump had been fatal.

CAN YOU "HANDLE" THE TRUTH?

y Thursday, September 7, more than 500 people had died in Soho, in an area of only a few blocks. An emergency meeting of the parish council was called, and worried men in dark suits gathered in the parish hall to discuss what measures they could take to try to halt the deaths and suffering.

Various solutions were suggested, such as burning sulfur in the streets to disinfect the air. Then a stranger, sitting alone in the back of the hall, asked permission to speak. The council members listened in astonishment as Dr. John Snow laid out the results of his door-to-door research. The council was skeptical about Snow's outlandish water theory. However, they reasoned that preventing people from drinking the Broad Street water could do no harm. The next day, workmen were sent out with instructions to remove the handle of the Broad Street pump. The spread of cholera, which had already been declining in the neighborhood, stopped altogether. The epidemic was over.

But the Soho Parish Council and the London Board of Health were still not convinced. It did look as though the water had had a role in spreading the disease, but perhaps the bad air had contaminated the water. And Snow hadn't proven to them that the well was the original source of the epidemic. They asked him to do more investigation and report back to them.

One man from the council volunteered to assist Snow with his investigation. But he wasn't an ally, at least at first. Henry Whitehead was the new assistant curate at St. Luke's, the local church, and had decided to get involved because he was convinced Snow's theory was just plain wrong.

THE PICTURE COMES INTO FOCUS

Despite their differences, the shy doctor and the young minister made a good team. Whitehead was just 29 years old, and St. Luke's was his first parish. He was full of energy and already knew many of the residents of Soho by name. Day after day he paced the streets, knocking on doors, trying to track down residents who had fled the neighborhood in the early days of the outbreak. He visited some homes four or five times, until he was satisfied that he'd gathered all the information he could.

While Whitehead walked the streets, Snow spent hours every night in his study, poring over the data they'd collected. Frustratingly, there seemed little left to learn. Then one night, Snow tried something new. He took his list of confirmed cases of cholera and transferred the information onto a map of the neighborhood. He drew a black bar for every case reported from each address. Soon there were clusters of black bars up and down the winding streets. He studied the map, pondering what it showed and what was missing.

Then he picked up his pen and marked in the locations of all the water pumps in the neighborhood.

By the time he put his pen down, he'd drawn a picture of the epidemic. The black bars radiating out from the location of the Broad Street pump were testimony to the deadly effects of the contaminated well. He felt certain the map would make an impression on the council in a way his earlier lists and tables hadn't been able to. But he still faced a problem. Could this map also overcome his co-investigator's reluctance to believe him?

MAPPING OUTBREAKS

John Snow's map of the Soho cholera outbreak is still studied by students of epidemiology today. Snow pioneered mapping as a technique for demonstrating the linkages between disease outbreaks and risk factors in the environment. In the Soho epidemic, the biggest risk factor was proximity to the Broad Street pump, and the map was an efficient way of helping officials to see that, and to get them to take action to stop the outbreak.

Epidemiologists today map outbreaks with sophisticated software that allows them to track epidemics through both space and time, and to predict how fast and far an epidemic is likely to spread.

New technology will keep providing new opportunities. In 2012, a disease-mapping app for smartphones was developed by the National Institute for Health in Britain. Called ClickClinica, the app lets doctors record the symptoms of a patient they've just seen and the treatment they recommended. If enough doctors use it, ClickClinica could provide doctors and scientists with a real-time map of the outbreak of epidemic disease.

THE FINAL CLUE

e'll never know whether Snow's map alone would have been enough to convince Whitehead or the parish council. Because at almost the same time, Whitehead himself uncovered the last piece of the Broad Street puzzle. One evening, sifting through the piles of documents that now filled his study, the assistant curate's eyes landed on a single line that had until then escaped his notice: "Death from exhaustion, after an attack of diarrhea four days previous." It was little Frances Lewis's death certificate.

Until now, Frances's death hadn't been considered part of the cholera outbreak, but Whitehead realized immediately that she was one of its many victims. He was surprised that a young baby had withstood the illness for four days, when adults often died of the disease in a matter of hours. Four days. That meant Frances had taken ill before any other cases were reported. He looked again at the death certificate to be sure, and noticed the address: 40 Broad Street, right next door to the Broad Street pump.

Whitehead's hands, holding the death certificate, began trembling. His brain whirled, at last making the connections that had eluded him and Snow. Here was evidence of a case of cholera that had started *two days before* the general outbreak in the neighborhood, and it was very likely that the victim's diarrhea had been disposed of near the Broad Street pump, which was the connection between all the other cases in the epidemic. Had Frances's cholera-laden diarrhea contaminated the water of the Broad Street pump, and led to the outbreak? Whitehead got up. Despite the late hour, he knew Snow would want to hear about his discovery.

The next day, Sarah Lewis answered a knock to find two serious-looking gentlemen on her doorstep. They'd come, they explained, to ask about her baby's illness. When had Frances first gotten sick? Where did the family get their water? Where did their waste go?

Sarah showed them the cesspool opening at the foot of the stairs, where several times a day she had poured out the water she'd used for soaking the dirty sheets and diapers. Seeing that the cesspool was just steps away from the Broad Street pump, Snow knew that at last he had solid proof of the source of the epidemic.

TOOLS OF THE TRADE

THE SHOE-LEATHER METHOD

Today John Snow is called the father of epidemiology. In addition to mapping the Soho cholera outbreak, Snow was the first scientist to systematically study an outbreak of disease, looking for patterns and possible sources. Prior to Snow's methodical studies, doctors only gathered anecdotal information from the patients they treated, and they didn't compare that information with data collected from healthy people in the area to look for similarities and differences. Snow's method of going door to door in the area of the epidemic is now called "shoe-leather epidemiology," and it's still one of the most valuable ways epidemiologists have of collecting information.

THE DIRTY TRUTH

now and Whitehead made such a convincing case that the parish council ordered both the cesspool in front of 40 Broad Street and the well under the corner pump to be excavated. The engineers called in for the job noticed immediately that the brick lining of the cesspool had decayed, and the meter (three feet) of earth between the cesspool and the well was saturated with sewage. Anything going into the cesspool would find its way—and fast—into the water in the well. The cholera from Frances Lewis's diarrhea had traveled into the street's drinking water, setting off the epidemic.

To this day, no one knows how the six-month-old baby got cholera in the first place. But thanks to John Snow and Henry Whitehead, people came to understand how *Vibrio cholerae* from Frances's diapers infected an entire neighborhood. The epidemic was a terrible tragedy, but from it the world learned how future epidemics of cholera could be prevented.

A few years after John Snow's investigation, the city of London installed the modern world's first major sewer system. Under the direction of engineer Joseph Bazalgette, the city built 132 km (82 miles) of brick-lined sewers, transporting London's waste far down the Thames. It was one of the biggest civil engineering projects ever undertaken, and it made London the most modern city of the time. Cities throughout Europe and North America were soon following London's lead by building sewer systems to safeguard the health of their inhabitants.

CHOLERA TODAY

Think cholera outbreaks are ancient history? Think again. Between 1816 and 1923, cholera killed over 2 million people worldwide. The disease came in waves of pandemics, with just a few years of calm in between. Then, for over 40 years in the middle of the 20th century, cholera seemed to vanish. There's a fairly simple explanation: modern sanitation. As modern sewer systems and water treatment became the norm across the developed world, cholera had far fewer opportunities to spread. From being the scourge of cities across the globe, it went to being an almost unknown disease.

Until it came back.

A cholera pandemic started in 1961, and it's still going on. It began in Indonesia, spread across Asia, and has hit countries throughout South America and Africa. In 1994, a cholera outbreak in Rwandan refugee camps in Africa killed more than 23,000 people in just over a month. Most recently, the disease appeared in Haiti after that country was hit by an earthquake in 2010. So far it has killed 6,500 people there.

Preventing cholera is one of the main reasons that international aid organizations like Doctors Without Borders race to get safe water and food supplies to disaster areas. Cholera gets a foothold when natural disasters strike, or when war or instability pushes large numbers of people into crammed refugee camps. Wherever there are crowded living conditions, a lack of clean water and sewage disposal, and too few doctors, drugs, and hospitals, cholera has a chance to thrive.

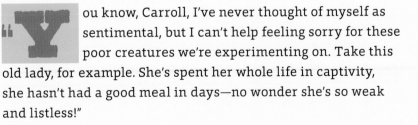

"DID THE MOSQUITO DO IT?"

YELLOW FEVER IN CUBA, 1900

You know, Carroll, I've never thought of myself as sentimental, but I can't help feeling sorry for these poor creatures we're experimenting on. Take this old lady, for example. She's spent her whole life in captivity, she hasn't had a good meal in days—no wonder she's so weak and listless!"

As he spoke, Dr. Jesse Lazear lifted a test tube up to the light and tapped it gently, dislodging the mosquito inside from her perch on the side of the tube. Briefly, the insect lifted into the air, but she soon settled back down again to cling to the slippery glass walls of her prison, her wings drooping.

"You're right, Lazear," observed his lab companion, Dr. James Carroll. "That little skeeter looks like she's on her last legs. Not much pep left in her, is there?"

Lazear smiled, but grimly. "She's not going to live out the day, in my opinion. Unless, that is, somebody can tempt her to feed on them. She bit a fever patient 12 days ago, and she's had nothing since then. She couldn't muster the energy to bite this morning's volunteer. I need another willing victim."

The two men looked at each other across the battered wooden lab table. In the silence, even the trapped mosquito seemed to be waiting to hear what would happen next.

At last Carroll cleared his throat. "She'll die today unless she feeds, you say?" he asked.

"Yes, and she's almost the last hatched from that batch of eggs Dr. Finlay gave us. When they're gone, I'll have to find more eggs and raise the insects from larvae again—and it's such a chore, Carroll! But the worst of it is that it will set our experiments back by days, waiting for new mosquitoes to reach maturity."

Carroll took a deep breath and started rolling up his shirt sleeve. "Bring that test tube over here, and we'll see if her ladyship likes the taste of me."

When his friend hesitated, frowning uncertainly, Carroll laughed. "Come on, Jesse. You know as well as I do that yellow fever isn't transmitted by mosquitoes. That little imp is going to do nothing more than give me an itchy lump for a day or two. Then we'll be able to stop these foolish experiments and get back to the real work—finding the bacteria that causes the disease."

Reluctantly, Lazear picked up the test tube, pulled out the stopper, and jammed the mouth of the tube against his friend's bare arm. The mosquito fluttered aimlessly up and down, then came to rest again on the side of the test tube.

Lazear rolled his eyes, sighing in exasperation. "Just like this morning. Too weak to feed." He started to withdraw the test tube from Carroll's arm.

"Be patient, man! Give the lady a chance to make up her mind. Maybe she's picking out the tastiest spot."

After several minutes more of waiting and watching, Dr. Lazear gave up, leaving the test tube and its indecisive inhabitant to the care of Dr. Carroll. Carroll sat patiently holding the tube to his forearm, silently willing the mosquito to lift up from her perch. Finally he announced, "Success! She's done it, Lazear, she's done it!"

And that was the end of it. A few minutes out of a busy afternoon's work to make sure that an experiment stayed on schedule. Carroll had soon put the whole thing out of his mind. The bite didn't even itch.

THE CUBAN EXPERIMENTS

Why were these two doctors trying to tempt a mosquito to bite them? Although neither had much faith left in the experiment they were trying, they had come to Cuba a little over a month before in order to find the cause of yellow fever, one of the most feared and deadly diseases of the 19th century.

As their ship sailed into the great harbor of Havana, the capital city of Cuba, both Lazear and Carroll had been out on deck, eager to get their first sight of the famously beautiful island. Above the city rose green hills covered with waving palm and coconut trees, while the harbor was guarded by immense stone fortifications. Inside the city walls they could glimpse gaily painted homes, the tall spires of churches, and the elaborately decorated buildings that had given the city the name "Ciudad des las Columnas" (City of the Columns). But in the middle of the harbor, rising up out of the water, was a bare and blackened hulk that neither man could ignore.

It was the wreck of the *Maine*, a U.S. Army ship that had been blown up by the Spanish two years earlier, killing more than 260 sailors on board, and setting off the bitterly fought Spanish-American War. Lazear and Carroll had often heard the rallying cry echo through the United States: "Remember the *Maine*! To hell with Spain!" Now here it was before them, the ruined ship that had put their country at war—a war that had resulted in the victorious U.S. taking control of the Spanish island of Cuba.

In 1900, there were more than 50,000 American soldiers occupying Cuba, and the army was worried. The war might be over, but their troops were still dying—of yellow fever. In fact, already more soldiers had been lost to yellow fever than had been killed in the fighting. And with ships full of soldiers coming and going constantly between the island and the nearby American mainland, the risk of a sick soldier setting off an epidemic in an American city was growing by the day.

It was a risk the U.S. Army was determined to put a stop to. Terrible epidemics of yellow fever had ravaged cities across the United States all through the 18th and 19th centuries, with the sickness becoming known and feared as the "yellow death." During a single epidemic in Philadelphia, in 1793, 10 percent of the city's population had died. New Orleans was particularly unlucky when it came to yellow fever. That city had suffered six major epidemics by 1878, when it was hit again, along with 131 other cities and towns in the U.S. Nowhere, it seemed, was safe from the menace of the yellow death. But in Cuba, the U.S. Army was seizing the chance to solve the mystery of yellow fever, once and for all.

THE CUBAN TEAM ASSEMBLES

Along with Carroll and Lazear, the U.S. Army had ordered two other doctors to travel to Cuba: Major Walter Reed would lead the team, and Aristides Agramonte would assist him. All four were highly skilled doctors. Reed and Carroll were bacteriologists: specialists in uncovering the causes of disease, and in developing cures or treatments. The pair had worked together for several years at the U.S. Army Medical School in Washington, D.C. Lazear was the head of a clinical laboratory at Johns Hopkins University in Baltimore, and Agramonte was an experienced medical investigator. At Camp Columbia, the U.S. Army's main base in Cuba, the team's mission was simple: find the cause of yellow fever.

Simple, but incredibly risky. All four men knew that they were taking a terrible chance by agreeing to this assignment. Every year, especially in the rainy summer months, yellow fever took a terrible toll on the people of Cuba, killing hundreds or even thousands across the island. The first signs of yellow fever were chills, a crushing headache, and terrible pains in the limbs and back. Victims often showed a racing pulse and complained of stomach cramps in the early stages. Then fever set in, and the victim's temperature rose dangerously, sometimes to 40 degrees Celsius (104 degrees Fahrenheit) or more. Within days, the victim's skin and the whites of the eyes began to turn yellow, or jaundiced, as the disease attacked the liver—it was this frightening symptom that gave yellow fever its name. In the final stages of the disease, the victim began to vomit black, clotted blood. At that point, death was almost certain, although it could take up to two more weeks before the victim's suffering ended.

Yellow fever snuck up on its victims mysteriously. Did you get it from contact with a sick person's clothes or bedding? Did yellow fever germs travel from person to person through the air? Was it transmitted through contaminated water or food? Every doctor and scientist studying the disease had a favorite theory, and there was very little hard evidence for or against any of them. That's why Walter Reed was determined that his team would follow the strictest standards of scientific enquiry. Their experiments had to be foolproof, and their results had to stand the test of time. There had been other investigations into the causes of the yellow death, but Reed and his fellow doctors wanted theirs to be the last.

HOME AT CAMP COLUMBIA

In late June 1900, on the spacious veranda of their quarters at Columbia Barracks Hospital, the team met to plan their strategy. The summer rains were beginning, and soon the beds in the hospital would fill with patients. At Major Reed's suggestion, the four doctors decided they would start immediately, testing three theories about the transmission of yellow fever.

First, they were intrigued by the recent reports from an Italian researcher, Dr. Giuseppe Sanarelli, who claimed to have found a bacteria that caused yellow fever: *Bacillus icteroides*. To test his claims, the team would perform autopsies on yellow fever victims, remove tissue samples, and try to grow the bacteria from the samples. Carroll's skill as a bacteriologist would be essential to these experiments.

Another current theory held that yellow fever could be transmitted through infected clothing and bedding. Although the four doctors were more inclined to believe that a bacteria was the cause of the disease, they agreed to test this theory too. And for their third set of experiments, they decided to investigate a little-known theory from a doctor in Havana. For over 20 years, Dr. Carlos Finlay had been trying to prove that mosquito bites caused yellow fever in humans. Most people considered the theory too far-fetched, but Reed and his fellow doctors were determined to follow every lead they had. They would test Finlay's theory as well.

CURING YELLOW FEVER?

During the Philadelphia epidemic in 1793, over 4,000 people out of a population of 28,000 died of yellow fever in just three months. To help stop its spread, the city's doctors advised people to:

"Avoid fatigue of body and mind. Don't stand or sit in a draft, in the sun, or in the evening air."

"Dress according to the weather. Avoid intemperance. Drink sparingly of wine, beer, or cider."

"When visiting the sick, use vinegar or camphor on your handkerchief; carry it in smelling bottles; use it frequently."

"Place your patients in the center of your biggest, airiest room in beds without curtains."

"Stop building fires in your houses or on the streets. They have no useful effect. But burn gunpowder. It clears the air. And use vinegar and camphor generally."

INTO HAVANA

As soon as possible, the four arranged to visit Dr. Finlay at his home in Havana. They traveled in a horse-drawn *volante*, a type of high-wheeled carriage unique to Cuba, jolting along the rutted dirt roads into the city. None of them expected the Cuban doctor's theories to hold water. After all, Havana was a sleepy backwater: What kind of scientific research could be happening here?

The white-bearded, bespectacled Dr. Finlay welcomed them graciously, but there was little small talk among the five medical men that night. Finlay got right to the point.

"The question your team investigates, Dr. Reed, should not be 'what is the cause of yellow fever?' but 'what transmits it?'"

Dr. Finlay was already convinced of the answer to that question. He had conducted no fewer than 103 experiments, getting human volunteers to expose themselves to the bites of mosquitoes. But he had no training in designing experiments, and his results were ignored by the medical community because his volunteers hadn't been kept in isolation—they could just as easily have picked up yellow fever from another person as from a mosquito bite, the skeptics argued.

Finlay begged Reed and the others to complete the work he had started. He was convinced that one particular species of mosquito, the *Aedes aegypti*, spread yellow fever. He explained that when a mosquito "bites" a person, it actually pierces their skin with its proboscis, or long thin nose, to suck up blood—and in the case of a yellow fever patient, the blood would be infected with the germs that caused the disease. Then, when the mosquito bites someone else, those germs are transmitted into the new, healthy body, causing yellow fever.

As the team left, Finlay pressed a small bowl into Jesse Lazear's hands. "Mosquito eggs," he explained. "In two weeks, you'll have a lovely batch of insects to work with. Good luck." That night, back in their barracks, the four Americans lay awake for hours, each of them replaying Finlay's arguments in his mind. The next morning, they agreed: they would start investigating the mosquito theory immediately.

A few days later, the doctors made another decision. There was a problem they couldn't see any way around. In order to test Finlay's theory, they would need to raise the mosquitoes, have them bite patients suffering from yellow fever, and then have them bite healthy people in turn. If the theory was correct, though, their experiments would result in the test subjects developing yellow fever. They could not ask the soldiers at Camp Columbia or Cubans in the surrounding area to take such a risk, they agreed, unless they were also prepared to put their own lives on the line. Three weeks later, on August 27, Jesse Lazear put the mosquito on his friend James Carroll's arm.

TROUBLES ACCUMULATE

For three days Dr. James Carroll showed no effects from his mosquito bite. He carried on as usual, examining tissue samples under the microscope, looking for evidence of the *Bacillus icteroides* in yellow fever patients. Of all the team members, Carroll was the least convinced by the mosquito transmission theory. He was sure the answer to the yellow fever mystery would be found under the microscope, not by breeding insects.

HUMAN EXPERIMENTS

Walter Reed knew that to test the theory that mosquitoes transmitted yellow fever, he'd have to experiment on humans, and that some of them might die. He wanted every volunteer to understand the risks they were taking. The forms he asked all the volunteers to read and sign are among the earliest examples of "informed consent"—something that's now required in all human-subject experiments.

Sadly, not all experiments on humans have been as ethical. Following World War II, when the world learned that prisoners in Nazi Germany had been subjected to cruel experiments, the Nuremberg Code was developed. The international agreement states that researchers must have the consent of their subjects, and experiments must be well-designed and safe.

Even after this, however, researchers didn't always follow the rules. In an experiment conducted by the Tuskegee Institute and the U.S. Public Health Service, 399 black American farmworkers with syphilis were told that they were getting free medical treatment. Instead, the medical researchers simply observed them as they got sicker and sicker, in order to learn about the course of the disease. The study, which started in 1932, went on until 1972.

Today the World Medical Association publishes guidelines requiring scientific studies that involve human subjects to meet high standards of ethical practice. Ethics committees at universities and national research institutions scrutinize all research plans before approving them for funding, and the principle of informed consent that Walter Reed pioneered in Cuba is central to the design of every experiment that has human participants.

But on August 30 Carroll began feeling feverish. He and Lazear went for a swim that afternoon to cool off, but when Carroll emerged from the water, he started shaking, and soon he developed a blinding headache. Another army doctor looked him over and told him bluntly that he had yellow fever. Carroll didn't believe him, and he carried on working. Yet by the next afternoon, Carroll was lying in the yellow fever ward in Camp Columbia's hospital with a temperature of 39 degrees Celsius (102 degrees Fahrenheit), and there was no longer any question about what was making him so ill.

The research team was in shock, and unsure what to do next. Walter Reed had just returned to the United States to complete a research report on an earlier study he had been involved in. Lazear and Agramonte sent Reed a cablegram about Carroll. Overcome with guilt, Reed wrote to a friend, "I cannot begin to describe my mental distress and depression over this most unfortunate turn of affairs. We had all determined to experiment on ourselves & I should have taken the same dose had I been there. Can it be that this was the source of his infection?"

Fortunately, Carroll's case of yellow fever wasn't fatal. By September 6 it was clear that he was out of danger, and soon he was well enough to read a congratulatory letter from Reed: "Hip! Hip! Hoorah! God be praised for the news from Cuba today— Really I can never recall such a sense of relief in all my life, as the news of your recovery gives me!... God bless you, my boy." On the back of the envelope, Reed had hastily scribbled the question that was now foremost in all of their minds: *Did the mosquito do it?*

Though the evidence seemed to point to the weak old mosquito that Lazear had put on Carroll's arm, Carroll's illness wasn't proof enough that yellow fever was transmitted through mosquitoes. He could have been infected through his exposure to yellow fever patients in the hospital, or through his work with infected tissue samples in the laboratory. The research team needed more evidence: they needed to see if a mosquito could cause yellow fever in another volunteer.

But who would volunteer for such a hazardous duty? Carroll was now too weak, and the team suspected that both Agramonte and Lazear were immune. They knew that people who had survived yellow fever could not get the disease again, and Agramonte, who had been born in Cuba, might have had a mild case of the disease as a child. Lazear had already been bitten several times by infected mosquitoes without developing any symptoms. Reed was still away in the United States. The solution, as it turned out, stopped by their laboratory later that day.

Private William Dean was new to Camp Columbia, and to Cuba. He'd never been exposed to any yellow fever patients, and he was curious about the unusual experiments he'd heard were going on in the ramshackle laboratory. When Dean passed the door to the lab that day, he glanced in and happened to meet Lazear's eye.

"You still fooling with mosquitoes, Doctor?" Dean asked.

"Yes," said Lazear. "Will you take a bite?"

"Sure, I ain't scared of 'em."

A week later, Agramonte burst into the lab, startling Lazear with the news that Private Dean had been admitted that morning to the camp hospital with fever, chills, and a headache—the classic early symptoms of yellow fever. Could this be the evidence they needed?

HUMAN GUINEA PIGS

Private Dean's case of yellow fever was relatively mild, and he was soon on the road to recovery. With Carroll also slowly recovering from his illness, and the evidence against the mosquitoes mounting, everything seemed to be going well for the research team. Then, abruptly, disaster struck.

Jesse Lazear came down with yellow fever.

How had it happened? Dr. Lazear insisted it was accidental—he had been holding a test tube against a patient when a wild mosquito landed on his hand. Rather than swat the bug away and risk letting the captive mosquito escape, Lazear allowed the wild mosquito to bite him, feeling confident that he was immune to yellow fever. That's what he told his colleagues as he lay in his bed in one of the hospital's fever wards.

But later, as they were going through their research notes from the days before Lazear fell ill, Agramonte and Carroll came across a puzzling entry in Lazear's handwriting: "Sep 13: This guinea pig bitten today by a mosquito which developed from egg laid by a mosquito which bit Tanner Aug 6. This mosquito bit Suarez Aug 30, Hernandez Sep 2, De Long Sep 7, Fernandez Sep 10."

As Agramonte and Carroll well knew, there were no animals in their experiments. Who was the guinea pig Lazear had referred to? Could the note mean that Lazear had decided, on his own, to experiment on himself, allowing mosquitoes to bite him after feeding on fever patients? Before they could confront him with their suspicions, Dr. Jesse Lazear died of yellow fever, just 10 days after being bitten.

REED RETURNS

Walter Reed raced back to Cuba, only to find his research team in chaos. Lazear was dead, Carroll was still very weak from his bout of yellow fever, and Agramonte was deeply upset by what had befallen his colleagues. Yet despite all the suffering, important scientific work had been done—possibly enough to establish how yellow fever was transmitted.

Reed set to work immediately, interviewing Private Dean. In order to prove that the mosquito bite had led to Dean's illness, it was important to demonstrate that the bite was Dean's only exposure to the disease.

THAT BITES!

As anyone who's ever spent a hot summer night in a cottage, cabin, or tent can tell you, nothing keeps you awake at night like a mosquito buzzing in your ear. And the next day—boy, those bites really itch! Usually, the urge to scratch for a few days is our only lasting reminder of an unpleasant encounter with a mosquito. But if you're not so lucky, the effects of a mosquito bite can be worse than an itchy lump. Much worse.

In addition to yellow fever, mosquitoes spread a number of dangerous, even deadly diseases among humans. Depending on where you live, these include malaria, dengue fever, Rift Valley fever, West Nile virus, and encephalitis. And it is estimated that mosquitoes are responsible for transmitting these diseases to an astounding 700 million people every year.

Dean insisted that he hadn't left Camp Columbia and that he hadn't been in the hospital's fever wards. It looked like an open and shut case.

One month later, on October 23, Reed returned to the United States and delivered a report to the American Public Health Association, describing his team's experiments in Cuba and their conclusion: "The mosquito serves as the intermediate host [the carrier] for yellow fever." The medical community was unconvinced. A single case wasn't enough to prove anything, they told Reed. He needed to test and retest, and his experiments needed to be more carefully controlled, so that it was clear his research subjects hadn't been exposed to yellow fever other than through the mosquito bite.

The scientists who listened to Reed's report had been respectful, but there were others who didn't take him so seriously. An article in the *Washington Post* called Reed's mosquito theory "silly and nonsensical rigamarole." But the criticism and ridicule only made Reed more determined. He boarded a ship back to Cuba swearing that he wouldn't leave again until he'd proven beyond a shadow of a doubt that mosquitoes spread yellow fever.

"$100 IN AMERICAN GOLD"

Back at Camp Columbia, the research started again. Reed convinced the military governor of Cuba, Major General Leonard Wood, to give the team $10,000 to fund their experiments—the equivalent of nearly a quarter of a million dollars today. With the money, Reed had special cabins built away from the rest of the camp. He planned to keep the research subjects there in isolation for the duration of the experiments. The new research area was called Camp Lazear, in honor of Jesse Lazear's sacrifice. But the research team still hadn't decided one thing: Who would participate in the experiments?

The three remaining doctors talked it through again and again. Despite the dangers, it still seemed as if the only way to solve the mystery was to use human volunteers. This time around, though, they would make sure that everyone who volunteered was fully aware of the risks—including death. In addition, all the participants had to be young (because yellow fever was more dangerous in older people), healthy, and single (so that the experiments would not create any widows or orphaned children).

Men who agreed to participate in the experiments would earn $100 in gold. If they got sick with yellow fever, they would get another $100. For the U.S. soldiers, and for the poor Cubans and many impoverished Spanish immigrants in the area, it was a tempting offer. Soon, the research team had enough volunteers willing to sign their detailed consent form.

On November 20, work got underway in Camp Lazear. The camp was nothing more than an empty stretch of land outside Camp Columbia, where Reed had tents erected for the researchers and personnel, near the two wooden cabins where the subjects would stay while the experiments were carried out. No yellow fever had ever been reported in the immediate area, and Reed had it surrounded with barbed wire to create a quarantine zone.

On November 30, the researchers embarked on the first experiment, designed to test whether yellow fever could be transmitted through clothing and linen. Three volunteers donned nightclothes and underwear that had been worn by yellow fever patients, and they slept in beds covered with sheets and blankets from the fever hospital. Neither the clothing nor the sheets had

CLARA MAASS: VOLUNTEER OR VICTIM?

Most of the people who volunteered to take part in the Walter Reed's experiments on yellow fever were men—either private soldiers or local Cuban laborers. The lure of $100 in gold was enough to overcome their fear of getting yellow fever. And they were assured of good medical care if they did get sick during the experiments, which was more than they could expect if they contracted the disease on their own.

But there was at least one woman who volunteered to take part in the experiments: Clara Maass. And she wasn't doing it for the money. Clara was an army nurse who had served in the Philippines and in Cuba, seeing firsthand the terrible ravages of yellow fever. She decided to participate in the experiments because she wanted to join the fight against the disease.

Clara was bitten by a mosquito that had fed on yellow fever patients. She developed a mild case of the disease, from which she recovered. Then, several months later, she agreed to be bitten again, to test whether she had developed an immunity to the disease. She hadn't. Clara Maass died of yellow fever in the summer of 1901.

Her death caused a massive public outcry in the United States, and put an end to yellow fever experiments using human subjects. But as a nurse, Clara Maass understood the risks she was taking. She wanted to be part of the effort to stop yellow fever, even if it meant she lost her own life.

been washed—they were still covered with urine, feces, vomit, and blood from the terribly sick people who had used them last. For three weeks, the men stayed in the cabin. At the end of that time, no one had developed yellow fever.

Reed repeated the experiment three times, using different volunteers, and got consistent results. Each time, the men emerged from their three-week ordeal free from yellow fever. Reed had proven that one of the most widespread beliefs about this disease was wrong.

Immediately he embarked on the next experiment. One of the research cabins had been constructed with a fine wire mesh screen running down the middle, splitting the interior into two isolated halves. On December 21, the researchers released 15 mosquitoes that had previously bitten fever patients into one half of the cabin. A volunteer was admitted into the midst of the buzzing insects. At the same time, by a separate door, two other volunteers entered the adjoining section of the cabin—the mosquito-free zone. The three men stayed in the cabin, together yet separated, for two days. During that time the unlucky man in the mosquito zone was bitten again and again.

After two days, the bitten man returned to his tent while the two other volunteers stayed on in the cabin. The doctors closely monitored the bitten volunteer. On Christmas Day, Walter Reed stopped by the man's tent to check on him. The volunteer, Private John Moran, was lying in bed, his face flushed, his temperature a scorching 39 degrees Celsius (103 degrees Fahrenheit). He had yellow fever.

The two volunteers in the mosquito-free zone remained completely healthy. Victory! Because all the men had been kept in isolation throughout the experiment, it was clear at last that mosquitoes transmitted yellow fever between humans. Luckily, Moran made a complete recovery, so no lives were lost due to the experiment.

YELLOW FEVER TODAY

Thanks to Walter Reed's work in Cuba, yellow fever epidemics in much of the world are now a thing of the past. Preventive measures like screens and bug repellent keep people from getting bitten as often, and the growth of cities and the draining of swamps and marshes means there are fewer areas for mosquitoes to breed. But in large parts of South America and Africa, the disease is still a threat. Fortunately, there are vaccines.

In 1936, Dr. Max Theiler, a virologist working at the Rockefeller Foundation in New York, developed the first successful vaccine against yellow fever. Over the next 10 years, the Rockefeller Foundation produced more than 28 million doses of the vaccine, which they distributed around the world—helping to put an end to the fear of the yellow death. Theiler, who caught yellow fever himself while working on the vaccine, but luckily survived, won the Nobel Prize for Medicine in 1951 for his achievement.

PANAMA CANAL

The Panama Canal is one of the world's most important shortcuts, giving ships a quick way to get between the Atlantic and Pacific Oceans, without having to go all the way around South America. Nearly 14,000 ships use the 80-km (50-mile) canal every year. It's hard to imagine today, but the canal nearly didn't get built—because of mosquitoes.

The Panama Canal cuts through the country of Panama, which sits in the narrow isthmus of land between North and South America. The region is hot, swampy, and rainy for much of the year: perfect breeding ground for mosquitoes. From 1881, when a French company first got the idea to build a shipping canal from one side of Panama to the other, until 1889, when they gave up after repeated attempts, mosquitoes ruled the country. Over 22,000 French workers are estimated to have died of yellow fever and malaria during that time.

The United States was the next country to try its luck. Because Walter Reed and his team in Cuba had recently proven that mosquitoes transmitted yellow fever, the U.S. had a much better chance of success. In 1904, the Americans sent in teams of sanitary workers to drain swamps and ditches along the proposed canal's route (getting rid of the standing water where mosquito larvae hatched) and to fumigate areas populated by adult mosquitoes. A U.S. engineering team installed window screens and mosquito netting in the dormitories built for laborers, and they were quick to isolate anyone who became sick in special quarantine hospitals.

These methods worked. The canal took 10 years to build, and opened for shipping traffic in 1914. Even with all the precautions, though, 5,600 canal workers lost their lives to disease and accidents.

TRACKING THE SOURCE

Although Reed, Carroll, Lazear, and Agramonte proved that yellow fever was spread from infected people to healthy ones through the bites of mosquitoes, there was an even deeper mystery they weren't able to solve: Where did the disease come from in the first place?

Today we know that yellow fever is "endemic" among monkeys in the jungles of Africa. That means it's always present in the monkey population. Mosquitoes spread the disease among monkeys too. However, because there weren't large cities or dense populations of humans in Africa, yellow fever didn't reach epidemic levels there until slave traders entered the picture. Then, scientists think, the disease became a hitchhiker, traveling from Africa to the New World on slave ships in the 16th, 17th, and 18th centuries.

Mosquito larvae in water barrels on board the ships hatched and bred during the journey, spreading the disease among the prisoners crowded into the holds. When the ships arrived in America, for instance, and the passengers were sold as slaves, yellow fever spread quickly among people living in the coastal cities. In those days before screens, air conditioning, and bug spray acted as barriers between mosquitoes and humans, epidemics of yellow fever were a regular and terrifying feature of summer in the city, all the way from Florida up to Boston and New York.

James Carroll and Aristides Agramonte worked on yellow fever for the rest of their lives, searching for the germ that caused the disease. But it wasn't until 1927 that scientists using electron microscopes identified the virus that is the source of yellow fever.

A SPECIAL GUEST OF THE CITY OF NEW YORK

TYPHOID IN 1906

"**O**h, Cook, I just had to come and talk to you about this evening's dinner." Mrs. Warren was rarely seen in the kitchen of the family's grand rented summer house at Oyster Bay, Long Island, and when she did appear, the cook noticed that it always caused a commotion among the staff.

Not surprising, really. Mary had worked for many wealthy families over the years, and in her experience the lady of the house generally came to the kitchen only to complain. She'd been cooking for the Warren family in this fashionable summer resort town for almost three weeks now, so she was probably overdue for a scolding. The clams she'd served tonight— had they smelled a little off? Rich New York City folks could be terribly sensitive, she knew that.

Mary hoped she wasn't going to be fired—it had been hard enough finding this job, and she didn't look forward to the thought of pounding the pavement to look for work again so soon. But to her relief, she realized Mrs. Warren had come to the kitchen to praise her: "The clams were so tender—sublime! And the dessert! So refreshing, just the thing for a warm summer evening. My daughters were in heaven. What do you call that dessert?"

"It's Peach Melba, ma'am. Very fashionable just now. All the best New York restaurants are serving it. Named for a famous singer, they say."

"Peach Melba. How wonderful! You must make it for us again one evening before we return to New York. I am very pleased with you, Cook, and I intend to keep you on in the fall. I imagine that suits you?"

"Yes, ma'am. Thank you, ma'am."

"Fine. Good evening, Mary."

A SHAMEFUL DISEASE

The Warrens' cook, Mary Mallon, went to bed that night glad to have a steady job for the fall and winter. She would happily please her employers with more special desserts. A peach pie, perhaps?

But there would be no more elaborate meals cooked for the Warren family that summer. A few days later, on August 27, 1906, the household awoke to turmoil: Margaret, one of the Warrens' daughters, was seriously ill.

Margaret had gone to bed early the night before, complaining of a bad headache. By morning the headache was worse, and soon she was doubled over with stomach cramps and a terrible feeling of weakness and fatigue. As the day wore on, Margaret developed a violent cough, and her mother noticed that the girl's skin was hot and dry, almost burning to the touch. Her fever mounted, despite everything they could think of to cool her down.

That afternoon, one of the maids collapsed with fever. Then the gardener drooped over his rake, and he too had to be helped into bed. By the evening, the Warrens' second daughter had joined her sister in the sickroom. Finally, Mrs. Warren herself was stricken.

More than half the members of the household were now fighting for their lives. Doctors were called in, first from the nearby town, then specialists from New York City. Private nurses in white uniforms whisked down the corridors, carrying cups of broth on silver trays. The shades were pulled on all the windows, signaling to the neighbors that there was illness in the house. There were grave faces, and whispered conferences between the medical men. Finally, the diagnosis was delivered.

Typhoid fever.

Typhoid! It was unthinkable. Wealthy New York bankers' wives and daughters were not supposed to get typhoid, not in 1906. Not in fashionable resort towns like Oyster Bay, Long Island. Typhoid was a disease of the poor. It meant you didn't have proper standards of hygiene in your home. Immigrants, laborers, servants—those were the people who fell ill with typhoid, not the rich and privileged.

Outraged by what had befallen his family, Charles Warren contacted the owner of the summer house, demanding an explanation. The landlord, George Thompson, was concerned. If his luxury summer house got a reputation for harboring disease, how on earth would he rent it out next year? If people in New York heard that typhoid was running rampant in Oyster Bay, it could hurt the whole town. And he had four other houses to rent each summer. This mystery needed to be cleared up, quickly and discreetly.

Thompson started asking around, looking for an investigator with a scientific or medical background. It wasn't an area many people specialized in at the time, but eventually, more than three weeks after the Warren household members first fell ill, Thompson found just the man for the job: George Soper.

Soper was a sanitary engineer by trade. That meant he was an expert in the design and management of sewer systems, and, just as importantly, an authority on the transmission of disease through water contaminated by human waste. Soper had made a name for himself by tracking down the source of a typhoid epidemic in Ithaca, New York, a few years earlier. Now, he packed his bags for Oyster Bay.

Soper checked the plumbing in the Warrens' house by putting dye into the water in the toilet, to see if it showed up in the home's drinking water. The water from the taps remained clear and colorless. Next he looked at the home's cesspool: it was solid. Contaminated milk was a frequent source of typhoid, yet the dairy that supplied the Warren family was spotlessly clean. One by one Soper eliminated the usual suspects for a typhoid outbreak. He knew there had to be a source, but finding it wasn't going to be as easy as he had hoped.

MILK

Soper interviewed all the family members and the servants, trying to sniff out something unusual that might have happened in the days leading up to the August 27 outbreak. Someone recalled that they'd all eaten clams bought from a local woman on the beach. Soper checked, but none of the clam seller's other customers had gotten sick—it wasn't a case of contaminated shellfish.

Still, it made Soper wonder if something the family had eaten might have picked up contamination in the kitchen. He went back to talk to the kitchen staff, and that's when he learned something that made his ears perk up. The family had been having trouble keeping cooks that summer. The first cook had left in early August, and her replacement, hired just three weeks before the family got sick, had recently quit as well. The family was disappointed. They still had fond memories of that second cook's skillful way with desserts, which they described to George Soper in detail. As he listened to their praise of her Peach Melba, Soper found himself thinking that, with this mostly uncooked ice-cream-based dessert, "no better way could be found for a cook to cleanse her hands of microbes and infect a family."

New cook hired. Family gets ill. New cook leaves suddenly, without any explanation. It was highly suspicious behavior, in Soper's opinion. He asked for the cook's name.

"It's Mary. Mary Mallon."

TRACKING THE SUSPECT

 eorge Soper wasn't a professional detective. But over the next four months, his friends might have been forgiven for thinking he'd developed a striking resemblance to Sherlock Holmes.

Soper was obsessed with finding the mysterious Mary Mallon.

His first stop when he returned to New York City was at an employment agency that supplied the city's wealthiest households with servants. Did they have records for a cook by the name of Mary Mallon? Indeed they did. Working backwards through her employment history, Soper visited each of the families Mary Mallon had cooked for. Very quickly, a disturbing pattern emerged: "In every household in which she had worked in the last ten years there had been an outbreak of typhoid fever. Mind you, there wasn't a single exception," Soper wrote in the paper he later published about the case.

Mary, he discovered, was linked to 22 cases of typhoid and one death—all in wealthy homes with no previous history of typhoid. Yet how could this be? How could Mary have been ill and contagious with typhoid for 10 years? It didn't make any sense. Unless—and this is what had George Soper so intrigued—Mary Mallon was able to pass on the typhoid infection to others without showing any symptoms of the disease herself. Could Mary Mallon be a carrier?

In 1906, the idea of healthy carriers of disease was brand new, and very frightening. A German bacteriologist, Dr. Robert Koch, had recently published a scientific paper detailing his discovery of the first confirmed healthy carrier of typhoid. The carrier was a woman found working in a bakery in Germany, who had been ill with typhoid years before and then made a full recovery. The woman was perfectly healthy now, but feces, urine, and blood tests showed that she was still full of active typhoid germs, and her hand-washing was not careful enough. The result? Her customers were getting sick.

Could Mary Mallon be the first American healthy carrier of typhoid?

George Soper knew there was only one way to find out for sure: to have Mary tested. But where was she? He knew her history

THE DOCTOR'S PLAGUE

Clean hands are one of the most effective ways of preventing the transmission of communicable diseases—especially those that travel the oral-fecal route. But until not too long ago, even doctors didn't bother washing their hands.

In 1847, Ignac Semmelweis was a Hungarian doctor working at the maternity clinic of the Vienna General Hospital in Austria. At that time, 10 percent of women who came to the hospital to give birth died of childbed fever, also known as puerperal fever, a bacterial infection they developed after childbirth. Semmelweis suspected the doctors were passing the infection from woman to woman, and he asked his colleagues to try washing their hands in a water-bleach mixture before helping to deliver each baby. The rates of puerperal fever dropped to less than 2 percent. Semmelweis had no scientific evidence to back up his theory, though, and when he presented his findings to the hospital administration, he was fired. After he continued to argue that doctors needed to wash their hands, he was forced to leave Vienna, and he had difficulty finding work as a doctor ever again.

Twenty years later, when Louis Pasteur was able to provide scientific proof that microscopic organisms caused disease, Semmelweis's insistence that hand-washing could prevent illness began to seem more reasonable to the medical community. In the 1880s, Joseph Lister, a British surgeon, demonstrated that by sterilizing surgical instruments, the survival rate of patients increased dramatically. Medical practitioners quickly began to clean up their acts.

inside and out, but he still had no idea where the cook had gone after leaving the Warrens' house in early September.

It wasn't until the next spring—March 1907—that George Soper happened to hear about a family living on fashionable Park Avenue in New York City whose daughter was terribly ill with typhoid. He visited, introduced himself, and learned something very interesting from the distraught parents: just a few weeks before, they had hired a new cook. Yes, her name was Mary. Why yes, Mary Mallon—did Soper know her?

Soper probably ran all the way to the kitchen. He'd found the elusive Mary Mallon at last. But sadly, the interview he'd looked forward to for so long didn't go at all as he'd planned. In his eagerness to make an important scientific discovery, he overlooked the fact that he was dealing with a human being with emotions, not just a walking collection of typhoid germs.

When a stranger burst into her kitchen and demanded that she give him samples of her blood, feces, and urine, Mary was insulted and horrified. She did what any self-respecting cook would do: she grabbed the nearest weapon—a sharpened carving fork—and chased the madman out.

ROUND TWO

Unfortunately for Mary, that wasn't the end of it. Very soon, the authorities were knocking at her kitchen door.

Dr. Sara Josephine Baker was a medical officer with the New York City Health Department. Because she was one of the department's few women doctors, she was given the task of getting Mary Mallon to agree to provide

SARA JOSEPHINE BAKER: PUBLIC HEALTH PIONEER

Mary Mallon and her captor, Dr. Josephine Baker, had quite a bit in common. They were both single women struggling against the odds to make lives for themselves in New York City at the turn of the century. Dr. Baker—or Dr. Joe, as she preferred to be called—had the advantage of an education and a medical degree, but that doesn't mean she had it easy. In her first year as a doctor she made just $185—and she had to split that with another doctor who shared her office. Clearly, private practice wasn't the way to make it as a female doctor, and Baker needed to earn money. Her father and older brother had both died when she was a teenager, so she was responsible for supporting herself and her mother. She went to work part-time as a medical inspector, which is how she ended up searching for Mary Mallon.

Dr. Baker made many contributions to public health during her long medical career. She was especially interested in the connection between poverty and ill health. In 1907 Baker was put in charge of the city's new bureau of child hygiene, the first in the country. There, she developed policies and programs that were later picked up in 35 other states, including ensuring that all children received vaccinations, that free milk was available for children from low-income families, and that people looking after young children got training in the basics of infant care. By 1923, New York City had the lowest child mortality rate of any major city in the U.S., thanks to Dr. Joe's efforts.

Today, epidemiologists continue to explore the question of why some people are healthier than others, and what policy-makers and governments can do to ensure that all people remain as healthy as possible.

PUTTING DISEASE UNDER THE MICROSCOPE

When George Soper barged into Mary Mallon's kitchen and demanded samples of her blood, urine, and feces, she must have thought he was out of his mind. In 1907, laboratory tests to identify bacteria in human body fluids were still very new, and the idea that a doctor could diagnose a disease by looking at a tiny blood sample under a microscope sounded ridiculous to most people.

But George Soper's unusual request shows that he was familiar with the most cutting-edge medical developments of his time. Thirty years earlier, the bacteria that causes typhoid, *Salmonella typhi*, had been identified, and in 1892, New York City had set up the country's first bacteriology laboratory to investigate threats to public health. Soper knew that if he could take samples from Mary Mallon to the laboratory, he could immerse them in a growing medium (often beef broth was used) and within 48 to 72 hours, if her blood and urine contained typhoid, the bacteria in the samples would be visible under a microscope.

Using the newly developed techniques of bacteriology was particularly important for solving the mystery of the Oyster Bay typhoid outbreak: it was the only way to prove that Mary Mallon could have been the source. When Mary's fluid samples were analyzed, doctors found they were teeming with typhoid bacteria, even though she showed no symptoms of the disease.

the specimens they needed to prove she was a typhoid carrier. As Soper had already discovered, it wasn't an easy assignment. When Dr. Baker turned up, accompanied by two burly New York City policemen, Mary Mallon was suddenly nowhere to be found—and none of the other kitchen staff would tell them where she'd gone.

Baker and the police hunted through the home's closets and cupboards in search of the fugitive, and they were on the point of giving up when the doctor noticed a bit of colored cloth caught in a closed door. It was the edge of Mary Mallon's long skirt, giving away her hiding spot in a tiny cupboard under the stairs.

The doctor and the police had to haul the angry, fighting woman out of the house and into a waiting ambulance, ignoring the captive's protests that she wasn't sick, that she'd never had typhoid, that she'd never been so insulted in her life. Afterward, Dr. Baker remembered how "the policemen lifted her into the ambulance and I literally sat on her all the way to the hospital; it was like being in a cage with an angry lion."

Fecal, blood, and urine samples taken in the hospital confirmed what Soper had suspected. The city of New York had a typhoid carrier on their hands—now, what should they do with her? New York in the early years of the 19th century was trying desperately to clean up its act: clear the streets of garbage, manure, and sewage; establish safe drinking water supplies and sanitation for all its inhabitants; and reduce the rates of infectious diseases such as typhoid. In the early 1900s, 350,000 people in the United States became ill with typhoid every year. In New York City there were more than 4,000 cases a year.

Typhoid struck a few days after the victim ingested something contaminated with the typhoid bacteria, *Salmonella typhi*. A crushing headache was the first symptom, followed by fever, diarrhea, cramps, and fatigue. Patients were confined to bed for anywhere from two to six weeks, and during that time they were weak and vulnerable to other infections. Typhoid wasn't as deadly

QUARANTINE

It seems like an extreme solution, but quarantines, usually temporary ones, have been used to contain epidemics for centuries. The word comes to us from Italian and dates back to the time of the Black Death. In the 14th century, the Mediterranean port city of Dubrovnik required that all ships wait 40 days (*quaranta giorni*) before docking, to make sure that there was no plague among the crew that could be spread to the inhabitants of the city.

As the Black Death made its way through Europe, other cities began imposing quarantines, sometimes sealing off entire neighborhoods or towns. But as a method of disease control, it could easily backfire. Thousands of panicked people would flee infected cities, hoping to get out before quarantine orders shut them in with the sick and dying. Inevitably, some of these people would develop plague, spreading it far and wide.

Quarantine is still used today for diseases that are considered highly dangerous and for which no treatments exist. People who have been exposed to Ebola or anthrax, for instance, must be kept in quarantine until doctors are certain that the danger of their developing the disease has passed.

as the other waterborne disease of the time, cholera, but it was exhausting and dangerous. Without antibiotics to treat it, all doctors could do was to try to bring patients' fevers down, and make them as comfortable as possible.

The city's main weapons in their fight against disease were science and public health, and the health department was its warrior. Health inspectors had the right to march into homes to vaccinate people, to confine sick people to their houses, and—in extreme cases—to quarantine those who refused to comply with their orders. Clearly, Mary was a danger. She refused to believe that she was transmitting typhoid, and it would be too dangerous to allow her to continue working as a cook. But she hadn't broken any laws, so she couldn't be sent to prison.

The city's answer to this dilemma was to transport Mary from the hospital to an island in the middle of New York's East River. Since the 1860s North Brother Island had been used as a quarantine hospital for patients suffering from extremely dangerous or contagious diseases—smallpox, cholera, yellow fever, tuberculosis. Healthy, strong, able-bodied Mary Mallon was sent to live on the desolate, windswept island, with the sick and dying as her only companions. It must have seemed like a death sentence.

ROUND THREE

Over the next three years Mary Mallon spent her time writing letters, protesting that her civil rights had been ignored, and pleading for help to get her released from quarantine. Finally, she succeeded in having her case heard by the New York Supreme Court.

In the time that Mary Mallon had spent on North Brother Island, a surprising thing had happened: 50 other healthy typhoid carriers had been identified in the state of New York alone. Not one of them had been sent to North Brother Island. Health department officials were ready to concede that perhaps they had overreacted. Mary won her case, and her freedom, on the condition that she agreed not to work as a cook again. In 1910, after three years as a prisoner of the New York City Health Department, she was allowed to cross the river back to New York City.

The health department didn't see it as their responsibility to train Mary for new work. Instead, they helped her to get a job as a laundress—one of the hardest, worst-paid jobs available to a woman at that time. At first they checked in with her frequently. Then, as the weeks and months passed, less and less regularly. Finally, they lost contact with Mary altogether. What was she doing? Where was she living? It seemed no one cared any longer about the healthy carrier who had caused such a stir only a few years before.

Then, in 1915, a New York City maternity hospital had a serious outbreak of typhoid. Twenty-five doctors and nurses were taken ill. Two died. The hospital employment records showed that a new cook had been hired just weeks before the outbreak. The head of the hospital put two and two together and phoned George Soper. He showed Soper a sample of the hospital cook's handwriting. Said Soper afterward, "He handed me a letter, from which I saw at once that it was indeed Mary Mallon."

Soper contacted Sara Josephine Baker, who visited the hospital and recognized Mary Mallon immediately. "Sure enough," Baker later wrote, "there was Mary, earning her living in the hospital kitchen, spreading typhoid germs among mothers and babies and doctors and nurses, like a destroying angel."

The health department returned Mary to her quarantine on North Brother Island, and that's where she stayed for 23 years—until her death in 1938.

AMERICA—THE LAND OF OPPORTUNITY?

For the hundreds of thousands of poor Irish immigrants who came to the U.S. from the mid-19th century on, opportunity was what they sought. People left Ireland in droves because of the potato famine that devastated the country, and in cities like New York they joined thousands of other penniless, hopeful immigrants from Germany, Italy, and Russia. New York soon became the United States' most diverse city, but also its most unhealthy.

Tenements, or large apartment buildings—sometimes known as rookeries—were hastily built to offer cheap housing to immigrants. The apartments had no running water, and the buildings weren't connected to the city's sewer system. The result? Frequent epidemics of disease, which easily spread to the more well-off citizens too. Soon, immigrants began to be associated in some people's minds with dirt and disease. It made their lives even harder.

VILLAIN OR VICTIM?

From the beginning, newspapers had a field day reporting on Mary Mallon's case, and when an article in the *Journal of the American Medical Association* in 1908 referred to her as "Typhoid Mary," the tabloids immediately started using that name too. Before long, Typhoid Mary was a household name. Today, Typhoid Mary refers to anyone who, intentionally or not, spreads disease.

One of the reasons Mary Mallon's story is still so fascinating is that there are so many unanswered questions about her. Did she suspect, before George Soper first approached her, that she might have had something to do with the typhoid that struck all the families she worked for? Why did she risk going back to cooking after she'd finally won her release from North Brother Island? Re-creating her story in articles and books and plays and movies, people have tried to make up their minds about Mary. Was she a villain? Or was she just an ordinary person whose life was ruined by an uncaring system?

Mary was a woman, a servant, an Irish immigrant to the United States, unmarried, and with little education. All those things meant she had no power in the society in which she lived. Yet she wasn't afraid to chase officials away, elude doctors, fight the police, swear and argue, and write angry letters until the courts were forced to take notice of her. Doctors and officials were no doubt surprised to see Mary standing up for herself so fiercely, and her behavior may have branded her as a problem case in their eyes.

There's another reason Typhoid Mary's story continues to interest people: it raises questions about how far governments should go when trying to protect the public from epidemics.

Was it fair to keep Mary Mallon in isolation for so long? Toward the end of her life, Mary wrote, "I have been in fact a peep show for Everybody, even the Interns come to see me and ask about the facts already known to the whole wide world... Dr. Park even had me Illustrated in Chicago... I wonder if he would like to be insulted, and... called Typhoid William Park."

TYPHOID TODAY

I f you're lucky enough to live in a city with a working sewer system and a reliable supply of clean drinking water, chances are good you've never even heard of typhoid fever. In most of North America and Europe, typhoid is a disease of the "bad old days," before engineers, public health doctors, and city planners figured out how to safely dispose of the huge volumes of human waste generated by cities full of people. Sadly, for many people in other parts of the world, typhoid is still a terrifying reality.

The World Health Organization estimates that 22 million people get sick with typhoid every year, and 216,000 of them—mostly children—die from the disease. There are vaccines that can prevent typhoid, but for many of the Asian and African countries where typhoid is most common, the cost of introducing a vaccination program is too high—as are the costs of ensuring that poor people have clean drinking water.

"SEND THE WORD TO BEWARE"

THE SPANISH INFLUENZA PANDEMIC, 1918–19

Over there, over there
Send the word, send the word over there
That the Yanks are coming
The Yanks are coming...
And we won't come back till it's over
Over there.

More than 20 soldiers, all singing at the top of their lungs, made the popular song's lines echo down the long barracks building, ending with a shout on the last two words—*over there!*— that practically set the windows rattling in their frames. Albert Gitchell's head ached. Miserably, he pulled his thin blanket over his head and burrowed down in his bunk, trying to block out the noise and get some sleep. Here in these giant drafty barracks, hastily built only months before to house American soldiers on their way to Europe to fight in World War I, there was no escaping the rowdy songs and laughter that sometimes seemed to go on all night.

There was good reason to stay up singing: it was the only way to stay warm through the frigid Kansas night. Huddled around the glowing stove, clapping hands, stomping feet, sharing cigarettes, the men were able to keep the cold at bay. Normally, Albert would be in the thick of the fun, giving his renditions of all the popular tunes as loudly as he could. But tonight, he longed for quiet. More than anything, he wanted to go to sleep and wake up in the morning feeling less achy and feverish then he felt right now.

The winter of 1917–18 was the coldest on record in the state of Kansas, and the officers, who would normally order the soldiers to bed, took pity on the men crowded into Camp Funston. It was only the camp medical staff who got angry when they found clumps of men knotted around the stoves, and lectured the soldiers about the dangers of "spreading contamination." No one paid them any attention. The men needed to keep warm, and if that meant they risked spreading germs to one another, it was a risk they were prepared to take. After all, what was the worst that could happen—a couple of days in the infirmary?

One of the camp's superior officers had actually written a report for the army administration about the conditions at Camp Funston, complaining that "barracks and tents were overcrowded and inadequately heated, and it was impossible to supply the men with sufficient warm clothing." Nonetheless, training went on relentlessly.

Not quite a year earlier, on April 6, 1917, the United States had declared war against Germany, joining the Allied nations—among them England, France, Canada, Australia, and Russia—in the Great War, which we now know as World War I. But the country had only a small army, and they would need many more men to join the war effort. Within a few months, the army had drafted 2.8 million men, and massive camps were hastily erected all over the country to train the new soldiers before they were shipped overseas to the front lines of Europe.

Camp Funston, with its endless lines of tents and low wooden barracks on the enormous Fort Riley army reserve in Kansas, was one of the biggest. In March 1918, when Albert Gitchell was there, it housed 26,000 brand-new soldiers, who slept and ate and washed together in companies of 150 men—mostly in tents or barracks that had been designed for far fewer men.

The soldiers didn't stay long at Camp Funston. The camp was a depot, dispatching men out for further training at other camps across the United States, and to port cities such as Boston, where they would set sail for the battlegrounds of Europe. The U.S. planned to send 10,000 soldiers to France every day by the summer of 1918.

And although neither the men singing around the stove nor poor Albert Gitchell knew it, the United States would very soon be sending some invisible cargo to Europe along with its soldiers: a deadly virus.

THE WARDS FILL UP

Albert Gitchell woke up early. As an army cook, he was trained to wake in the pre-dawn hours, long before the reveille sounded, to report for breakfast duty. Today, March 4, he dragged himself out of his bunk and dressed in his uniform, even though his body screamed in protest and his head throbbed.

He made his way slowly across the frigid camp to the kitchens. By the time he arrived, the fires had already been lit. He slipped an apron over his head and took his place quietly in the line of cooks, hoping to avoid his sergeant's eye.

An enormous pot of porridge stood in front of him on the range, and he picked up a metal spoon to stir the mess and keep it from burning on the bottom. Nothing could make the men complain more loudly than burned porridge in the mornings—that had been one of his first lessons in the army.

Clang! The spoon slipped through his fingers and clattered noisily onto the rough wooden floorboards. Wearily, Gitchell bent down to retrieve it, then turned back to the vat on the stove.

"Private Gitchell! Stop what you're doing right now!"

Albert froze, the spoon in the air above the porridge. It was the sergeant.

"Gitchell, have you or have you not been instructed in the basics of kitchen hygiene?"

"I have, sir," Albert said.

"Then you know better than to use a dirty spoon from the floor. That's the fastest way to get the health officers in here, Gitchell, and we don't want them looking over our shoulders!" As he spoke, the sergeant strode across the kitchen until he was next to Albert. He noticed the young soldier was pale, his eyes glazed. Beads of sweat dotted his forehead. "You feeling okay, Gitchell?"

"Little... under the weather this morning, I guess. Didn't sleep too good," Albert replied dully.

The sergeant sighed with irritation. "Hygiene again, Gitchell. Kitchen staff are not to report for duty when sick. Take off that apron and get yourself to the camp hospital."

By the time he had crossed the camp to the hospital Albert was feeling worse—much worse. The medical officer didn't need to do much more than glance at him before making a diagnosis: "Flu. Report to the contagious ward. You're confined to bed, soldier."

Albert was barely out the door when another man staggered into the hospital. It was Corporal Lee W. Drake of the First Battalion's Transportation Detachment, complaining of headache, fever, sore throat, and aching joints—symptoms identical to Albert's. He was sent to join Albert in the contagious ward. So was Sergeant Adolph Ruby, right behind Drake, also suffering from flu symptoms. Another man followed, then another. The medical officer picked up the phone to alert the camp's doctor about the sudden rash of influenza cases.

When the doctor arrived, he was staggered to see a line of sick men that stretched out the infirmary door and across the hospital grounds. That evening, poor Albert Gitchell was kept awake by noise again—not rowdy singing, but coughing and moaning from the more than 100 fellow sufferers crowded into the contagious ward of the hospital with him. By the end of the week there were 500 soldiers confined to bed with influenza at Camp Funston.

PRIVATE GITCHELL, PATIENT ZERO

Private Gitchell, army cook, became the first recorded patient in the great influenza pandemic that over the next year would kill between 50 and 100 million people around the globe. Albert survived his bout of the flu, but he was one of the lucky ones. At Camp Funston, 48 of his fellow soldiers died from influenza that month, and as the great movement of U.S. troops began, sick men from Funston spread the disease to other camps.

A VIRUS THAT GETS AROUND

Spanish influenza moved so fast in 1918 that there were rumors the disease was a "secret weapon" being spread by the German army. Another rumor was that the seeds of the disease were contained in the poison gas used on the battlefields.

We know now that influenza is spread through infected droplets in the air. People with influenza "shed" the virus for three to six days after being infected, often before they have developed any symptoms. And the virus is tough: it can survive on a hard surface like a doorknob for up to two days, waiting for a hand to help it make the leap to a mouth or an eye or a nose. It is a disease so perfectly adapted to crowds that one sneeze can infect dozens of people.

In March 1918, 84,000 American soldiers set sail for the port of Brest, in France. In April, 118,000 more boarded troop ships for the journey to the front lines. Influenza spread fast in the crowded ships, and hundreds of men had to be carried off when they landed in France. Thousands more were still walking, but extremely infectious.

The Allied soldiers already in Europe were in weak condition after four years spent in the trenches. Among these men, the influenza virus spread like wildfire.

Tens of thousands of soldiers began filling army infirmaries in the late spring of 1918, too sick to report for duty. And while most were up and around again within a few days, the sheer number of sick men affected military operations. The British navy had to delay launching its fleet for three days that June because there weren't enough healthy sailors available to man the ships.

Soon the virus crossed the no-man's land between the trenches and began spreading among the German troops. For months, Germany had been planning a massive offensive for the spring of 1918, but with tens of thousands of sick soldiers, that operation had to be cancelled. Many historians now believe that if influenza hadn't prevented Germany from launching its offensive, Germany might have won the war.

Still, nobody outside the army knew that one of the biggest epidemics in human history was underway. Almost every country had a wartime censorship law that put restrictions on what newspapers and radio stations could report. Printing or broadcasting any news that could hurt the war effort or damage public morale—making people worry that their own country wasn't going to win the war—was forbidden. So letting people know that hundreds of thousands of soldiers were sick was definitely off limits.

IT WASN'T
"JUST THE FLU"

Doctors had never seen anything quite like Spanish influenza.
Some of the first major outbreaks happened at military camps near
Boston in the early fall of 1918. In a letter to a friend, one camp
doctor described the horrors he was witnessing: "Two hours after
admission they have the Mahogany spots over the cheekbones and
a few hours later you can begin to see the Cyanosis [a condition in
which the skin turns blue from lack of oxygen] extending from the
ears and spreading all over the face, until it is hard to distinguish
the colored man from the white.

"It is only a matter of hours then until death comes and it is
a simple struggle for air until they suffocate. It is horrible. One
can stand to see one, two, or twenty men die, but to see these
poor devils dropping like flies gets on your nerves. We have been
averaging about 100 deaths a day, and still keeping it up... It takes
special trains to carry away the dead. For several days there were
no coffins and the bodies piled up something fierce, we used to go
down to the morgue... and look at the boys laid out in long rows.
It beats any sight they ever had in France after a battle."

That meant members of the public didn't take precautions that might have kept them from catching the disease, like staying away from crowds. Instead, people were encouraged to attend rallies and parades in support of the troops. The disease spread fast among the civilian population in Europe, eventually reaching Spain, where even the king came down with a case of influenza. Spain, unlike almost every other country in Europe, wasn't involved in the war. It was officially neutral, so its newspapers were free to print all the news. That spring, the big news in Spain was the influenza epidemic. Other countries, unable to report on their own epidemics, reprinted the articles about the outbreak in Spain, and so the disease that spread across the world came to be known as "Spanish influenza."

CALL IN THE SCIENTISTS

> BLACK DEATH

Soon, influenza was out of control, causing chaos and death around the world. And there didn't seem to be anything doctors could do to stop the spread of the disease or to help its victims. U.S. Surgeon General Victor Vaughan was quoted as saying that the doctors of the day "knew no more about the flu than 14th century Florentines had known about the Black Death."

It was a big setback. Until Spanish flu came along, medical science had been steadily conquering one disease after another. Cholera, typhoid, yellow fever, malaria: many of the terrifying diseases of the past could now be prevented and effectively treated. But suddenly influenza, which no one had taken seriously as a threat to human life, was decimating populations worldwide.

WILL THIS WORK?

Since doctors and scientists had no cure for Spanish flu, people turned to folk remedies to protect themselves. Garlic, mothballs, kerosene on sugar, powdered cinnamon, and eucalyptus oil were all popular preventives. People wore bags of camphor around their necks, carried potatoes in their pockets, and ate raw onions to try to repel the germs.

In the state of Louisiana, "sacred pebbles" supposedly blessed at a shrine in Japan were sold to ward off Spanish influenza. You could also try sprinkling sulphur on your shoes or inhaling the smoke from smoldering wet hay. Many people thought that smoking tobacco would help. One store in Holland made smoking compulsory for its employees.

Did any of these methods stop the transmission of Spanish flu? It's unlikely. In fact, by making people feel that it was safe to go out in public, folk remedies may have led to more people catching influenza.

A NEW SCIENCE FOR A NEW CENTURY

"You're an epi-what?"

Even today, epidemiologists are used to getting blank looks when they tell people what their job is. In 1918, Dr. Wade Hampton Frost's job description probably left most people scratching their heads. Epidemiology as a specialized discipline was brand new at the time, and almost unknown.

In Britain, the London Epidemiological Society had been founded in 1850 to study epidemics. Yet it wasn't until the 1880s that the first epidemiologists were hired in Britain to oversee public health and to investigate disease outbreaks. In North America, the process of recognizing epidemiology as a useful part of public health was even slower: it wasn't until 1902 that the U.S. Public Health Service was founded, and it was more than 10 years later that the first school of public health, at Harvard University, was established, in 1913.

When Wade Hampton Frost was asked to conduct studies on the 1918 influenza epidemic, it was a big step forward for epidemiology, as well as a step into the unknown. A study of the size and scale needed to understand the path of Spanish influenza through the United States had never been undertaken. Frost and his small team needed to develop methods for gathering and analyzing vast amounts of data, well before computers existed. Their success helped usher in an era of using epidemiological approaches to fight and prevent some of humanity's most feared diseases.

And it was happening with such lightning speed that there was almost no time for the scientific community to come up with solutions: no time to develop vaccines, no time to organize a worldwide public health response.

In the U.S., one team of scientists was working hard to analyze the spread of the disease and try to discover how it was spreading. On April 18, 1918, the head of the Public Health Service sent a letter to Dr. Wade Hampton Frost, asking him to take charge of the newly formed Office of Field Investigations of Influenza. It was a grand title for a small operation with very little funding. Dr. Frost had previously investigated typhoid outbreaks along the Ohio River and polio epidemics in New York. He was one of the most respected American scientists in the new field of epidemiology.

THE SECOND WAVE HITS

For Frost and his small staff—he had just one other full-time doctor working with him, and a few clerks and assistants—the task at first seemed overwhelming. Then, before they'd even been able to put together a research strategy, it looked as if their problems might be over. In early summer, the flu suddenly vanished—or seemed to. The hospitals and the army's infirmary tents were no longer overrun with flu sufferers, and life returned to normal for soldiers and civilians. But the reprieve was short-lived, because in fact the virus was mutating, or changing its form. It was soon to reappear as a much more deadly disease.

That fall, three epidemics of influenza exploded in the same week, in three cities around the world: in the African city of Freetown, Sierra Leone; in Brest, France; and in Boston, U.S. These three outbreaks launched the second wave of the pandemic. And this time, the virus was no longer just an extremely contagious three-day illness. During six terrible weeks in the fall and early winter of 1918, tens of millions of people would get sick, and millions of them would die of influenza.

All three cities were major transport hubs for the military. American troops passing through Brest picked up the virus and distributed it around Europe. Soldiers returning home to North America passed through Boston to board the trains that carried them—and the virus—to every corner of the continent. Ships on their way between Europe and battlefields in Africa and the Far East stopped in Freetown to take on coal to fuel their engines—and throughout the fall of 1918 they also brought along the influenza virus.

The pandemic caused a crisis in many countries because of the wartime shortage of doctors and nurses. In the U.S., a third of the doctors and nurses in the country were involved in the war effort, and those who remained to care for the civilian population were overworked and undersupplied. Even when a flu victim could find a doctor or an available hospital bed, there wasn't much that could be done to treat the disease. Doctors relied on rest, liquids, and hope to pull patients through. All too often, patients didn't make it.

No one had ever seen influenza like this before. Patients could develop any of an array of extreme symptoms: terrible pain, very high fevers, chills, earaches, headaches lasting for days, bleeding from the nose, mouth, ears, and eyes, vomiting of blood, and lungs so filled with fluid that patients almost literally drowned. Often, before death, patients turned blue from a lack of oxygen to the blood— what one doctor described as "a dusky, leaden hue."

The disease could overtake you so quickly there were reports of people dropping dead in the streets, and of people who went to bed at night healthy and were found in the morning stone-dead. There were stories of entire families falling sick, and of children left orphaned and alone in homes filled with the dead bodies of their family. Some cities ran out of coffins, so the dead had to be buried in mass graves. Horse-drawn wagons went up and down the streets, the drivers calling for people to bring out their dead. Scenes like these had not been seen since the days of the Black Death, when plague decimated the population of Europe.

As this new strain of flu swept the world, wartime media blackouts had to be abandoned. Across the United States, Canada, and Britain, governments and media warned people to protect themselves.

WHAT'S IN A NAME?

To Hungarians influenza was known as the "Black Whip." Germans called it "Blitzkatarrh" (lightning cold) or "Flanders Fever." In Poland it was known as the "Bolshevik Disease," and in Spain it was "Naples Soldier." People in Ceylon named it "Bombay Fever." The Swiss called it "La Coquette" (the courtesan). Italians knew it as "Sandfly Fever." To the Japanese it was "Wrestler's Fever," while in France it was "La Grippe" (the flu). But if you were British, Canadian, or American, the disease that had everyone terrified during the fall of 1918 was the Spanish flu.

The names might have been different around the world, but almost all of them had one thing in common: they pointed the blame for this dreadful disease at someone else.

Movie theaters, dance halls, libraries, restaurants, and churches—anywhere that people might congregate—were closed. Posters and signs advised people to cover their faces when coughing or sneezing, and many people took to wearing gauze surgical masks. But nothing, it seemed, could stop or slow down the spread of the disease. In Dublin, Ireland, public health workers poured huge amounts of disinfectant into the street gutters in an attempt to protect the city. New Zealand began to hunt down all the rats in its towns and cities, in case they were the culprits in spreading influenza. These and other misguided attempts had absolutely no effect on the pandemic.

Tragically, late that fall, the second wave of the pandemic got a huge boost from an unexpected event: the end of the war. When peace was declared at 11:00 a.m. on November 11, 1918, massive celebrations broke out all over the world. City centers were jammed with celebrating crowds, impromptu parades took place, people laughed and shouted and sang, they hugged and kissed and shook hands—and they spread influenza.

AN INFLUENTIAL REPORT

As the second phase of the pandemic started, Dr. Frost and his small research team struggled with a tidal wave of information. Data poured in from locations all over the world where influenza outbreaks were being reported. And there were major inconsistencies. In some cases, influenza was reported as a cause of death, while in others death was attributed to pneumonia. Were those deaths part of the pandemic too?

A DISEASE THAT CHANGED HISTORY

American president Woodrow Wilson came down with Spanish flu in March 1919, following World War I. Wilson was in Paris, meeting with the leaders of France, England, and Italy to decide on the terms of the peace treaty with Germany. France and England were demanding that Germany pay the costs of repairing their war-damaged nations. But Wilson was concerned that would destroy the German economy and push the country into chaos. The men spent weeks arguing and negotiating. Then Wilson got sick.

By the time Wilson caught Spanish flu, the most lethal phase of the pandemic was over. The virus had changed again, into a less dangerous form. Still, the U.S. president was extremely ill, and once he recovered he had no energy left to continue arguing. He agreed to the terms that France and England wanted and left for the United States as soon as possible. A few months later, he suffered a stroke and died, possibly still weakened from his attack of influenza.

Just as Wilson had feared, the heavy demands placed on Germany to pay war reparations caused economic upheaval in that country, creating conditions that historians now agree led to the rise of Adolf Hitler and the National Socialists, or Nazi Party, in the 1930s.

Part of the confusion came from the fact that U.S. doctors treating influenza patients in 1918 were not required to report the cases to the local board of health. Influenza, up until then, had not been considered a disease that the Public Health Service needed to track—unlike diseases such as smallpox, typhoid, or cholera, which they were very concerned about and kept close tabs on. Who had needed to track the number of cases of flu, which was usually a mild three-day illness?

For Frost and his team, this lack of information presented a major difficulty. How could they determine how widespread the disease was, or how lethal it was, without knowing how many cases there were? The only answer was "shoe-leather epidemiology," going house to house, knocking on doors, asking how many in each home had suffered the flu and how many had died. It was the same

IT'S A MUTANT!

Influenza is a master of disguise. And because the virus is so changeable, we get sick from it year after year. Each time a new strain emerges, our immune systems no longer recognize the virus, and new flu vaccines have to be formulated. Scientists call these changes to the virus "mutations."

Influenza viruses can mutate in two ways: through either antigenic *drift* or antigenic *shift*. (An antigen is any substance, like a toxin or a virus, that causes an immune response in the body.) Antigenic drift is a process of gradual change, in which the virus changes bit by bit. Antigenic shift is fast and causes big changes. Scientists speculate that antigenic shift caused the Spanish influenza virus to so quickly turn lethal in the fall of 1918.

technique that John Snow used in London during the 1854 cholera outbreak. Frost had conducted shoe-leather surveys in New York while investigating a polio outbreak in 1916. But how could one small office survey an entire country, much less the entire world, to track the course of a pandemic?

In the end, Frost knew he could only hope to survey a tiny sample. He and his team chose 10 cities, then trained hundreds of canvassers, who they sent out to interview the inhabitants. Over the spring of 1919, Wade Frost's surveyors talked to 112,958 people, asking them in detail about their experiences during the Spanish flu pandemic. Had they gotten sick? Did they know anyone, a friend or neighbor or family member, who had come down with influenza? How long were they sick for? What were their symptoms?

TOOLS OF THE TRADE

FINDING PATIENT ZERO

One of Dr. Wade Hampton Frost's biggest contributions to epidemiology had nothing to do with Spanish flu. In the 1930s Frost was in the U.S. state of Tennessee investigating tuberculosis, an infectious lung disease that even today kills millions of people worldwide. As he pored over the records of cases, Frost realized that when an outbreak could be traced back to a single individual, the full pattern of the outbreak could be reconstructed. Finding that person would allow epidemiologists to determine how the disease was spreading, how contagious it was, and what made people vulnerable to the disease. He called that person at the center of the outbreak the "index case." Epidemiologists still use the term, and the techniques that Frost developed to identify the index case. Today, the index case is often also called "Patient Zero."

In August 1919, Frost published a report entitled "The Epidemiology of Influenza." It is still studied by epidemiologists today, because of the discoveries that Frost and his team made—two in particular. First of all, the report noted that before anyone was aware of the influenza epidemic there had been a rise in the number of reported deaths across the U.S. from pneumonia. Since pneumonia is a lung infection that can result from influenza, an increase in pneumonia is one of the early warning signs of a flu epidemic that public health agencies still look for today. Second, Frost and his team discovered that influenza was particularly lethal among the elderly and the very young— which is why today flu vaccinations are given first to people over age 60 and under 5.

The 1918 influenza pandemic also killed an unexpectedly high number of healthy young people, and its path of destruction came to be known as the "lethal W," because charts of the death rates showed an alarming bump in the middle. Why did Spanish influenza kill so many people who were in the prime of life? It's a riddle that has continued to fascinate medical research-ers. Scientists now estimate that a similar strain of flu had not appeared for at least 70 years before the 1918 epidemic, so almost no one had any immunity to Spanish influenza. That meant that many more young adults came down with Spanish influenza than would be expected in a normal flu outbreak.

But this was no normal flu, either: it was deadly. Some researchers believe that the Spanish influenza virus was so particularly lethal to young people because it triggered an over-reaction in its victims' immune systems. The strong immune systems of healthy young people were turned into killing machines by the virus, causing such extreme symptoms that the sufferers eventually died.

COLD CLUES

For many years there was no way to study the virus that caused Spanish influenza. The mystery of what had made the disease so exceptionally lethal was buried along with its many victims. Then, in 1993, a young Canadian scientist named Kirsty Duncan, a medical geographer at the University of Windsor, started investigating the history of Spanish flu. By chance, Duncan heard about seven miners who had died in the Spanish flu pandemic in an isolated location in the far north: the Norwegian town of Longyearbyen. They had been buried in the

HOW MANY DIED?

Record-keeping around the world ranged from very basic to non-existent at the start of the 20th century, which means we'll never know precisely how many people died from Spanish influenza, or how many people caught the disease, either.

In India, estimates are that between 16 and 18 million people died. (Spanish flu also came hard on the heels of a plague epidemic that killed 12 million people in India between 1898 and 1918.) While there are no statistics available for Africa, estimates place the number of deaths in the tens of millions. There are no reliable statistics for the death tolls in Southeast Asia, China, or South America. In Canada, 50,000 people died from Spanish flu, while in the U.S. there were 550,000 deaths. In Britain 228,000 people died, in Germany 400,000, and in France 300,000.

permafrost—ground that remains frozen year round. Duncan got excited. Was it was possible the miners' frozen bodies had been preserved well enough that tissue samples could be taken? If so, maybe the deadly virus could still be identified.

Duncan consulted with the local community in Longyearbyen and the families of the miners. It was a long process, but once she had the permission to exhume the bodies (dig up the graves) she assembled an international team of scientists and researchers. Just as everything was set to begin, Duncan's team learned that researchers in the United States had taken tissue samples from the bodies of Inuit people in Alaska, who had also died in the pandemic and been buried in permafrost. In the race for scientific glory, the American team had pulled ahead. Kirsty Duncan was disappointed, and she was left with an ethical dilemma: If useful samples had already been found, should her expedition still go ahead?

In the end, Duncan's team did exhume the bodies of the miners. Unfortunately, the bodies had decomposed more than the team had hoped, and it was difficult to extract useful tissue samples. In 2005, the American researchers announced that they had successfully isolated the Spanish influenza virus from the DNA of an Alaskan Inuit woman who died during the pandemic. Their findings showed that the 1918 influenza was a type of avian (or bird) flu.

Scientists continue to study the Spanish flu virus, hoping to discover why it mutated into such a deadly form in the fall of 1918. Will the nearly 100-year-old virus yield information that could help prevent another massive pandemic? Only time will tell.

A GOOD HOST

Swine Flu: World on Alert! Fear of New Global Outbreak as Bird Flu Strain Found in Humans! Read the news these days and you're sure to see headlines like these about swine and bird flu. The most dangerous types of influenza for humans start out in animals and then change to become infectious to people.

We know now that Spanish influenza was a strain of avian (or bird) flu that spread to the human population. Wild aquatic birds are the "host species" for avian flu, which means that the virus is common among them and usually causes only a mild illness. But occasionally an infected wild bird may come into contact with a domesticated bird, like a chicken, and spread the disease. Avian flu can be lethal to chickens—and can sometimes make the leap from chickens to people, changing and spreading among the human population.

In the past 40 years, many flu epidemics have started in areas where people live in crowded conditions and in close contact with poultry. In 1997, the world panicked when thousands of chickens suddenly died at several poultry farms near Hong Kong, China. Soon, people in Hong Kong began getting sick, and public health officials worried that the world was on the brink of another lethal influenza pandemic. To try to stop the spread of the disease, all the poultry in Hong Kong and the surrounding area had to be killed— as many as 1.5 million birds!

Then, in 2003, outbreaks in Asia began again, and they continue today. Health organizations around the world are monitoring the virus closely. So far, the disease has only affected people who are in direct contact with poultry. But will the virus change and spread from human to human, starting another pandemic? That's the question that worries scientists.

MYSTERY IN THE JUNGLE

EBOLA IN ZAIRE, 1976

The room was stuffy and windowless. Paint was peeling off the walls, leaving damp, scabby patches of discolored plaster. But the floor was clean, and so was the narrow iron cot in the corner. A man lay on the cot, sweating. His eyes were glazed. The only sound was a faint wheeze as he panted for breath. Mabalo Lokela was very sick.

It was September 1976, and Mabalo was in Zaire, a country of steamy, sprawling jungle and congested cities in central Africa. Zaire, in 1976, was not a good place to be sick. There weren't enough doctors, or enough nurses or hospitals or clinics. Worst of all, there weren't nearly enough drugs to treat everyone needing medical help. Zaire (now called the Democratic Republic of the Congo) was a tropical country, where diseases spread by insect bites, parasites, or contaminated food and water were common. Since most of the country's citizens at that time were poor, living in crowded and sometimes unsanitary conditions, illnesses could spread like wildfire. In Zaire, getting sick was a fact of life—but getting well was not so certain.

The village of Yambuku, in Zaire's remote northern Equateur province, was a particularly unlucky place to fall ill. Yambuku was surrounded on all sides by jungle, hours away by rutted dirt road from the nearest town. The village had no doctors, and no real hospital—just a clinic run by an order of Catholic nuns from Belgium. But unlucky or not, that's where Mabalo found himself, because Yambuku was his hometown.

Mabalo was the village schoolteacher, and he was just back from one of the only holidays he'd ever taken. He had visited family and friends in surrounding villages, gone on a few hunting trips, done some sightseeing. But instead of returning home with a souvenir or two and some happy memories, he'd gotten a raging fever, a splitting headache, and a body racked with cramps. Malaria, he was pretty sure. Mabalo had been ill with malaria before. Mosquitoes bred in the low wet fields cleared for coffee plantations, and since no villagers could afford screens on their windows, everyone was vulnerable to the "shaking fever."

He lay in one of the Yambuku mission's few examining rooms. He hoped that the nuns might have some drugs left over from their last shipment of supplies from Europe. If luck was with him, he'd get a shot, go home, and hope that the fever receded enough so that in a week or two he could work again.

The nun who bustled in to treat Mabalo agreed that, yes, it seemed he'd got malaria again. Sister Beata wasn't a nurse—none of the missionaries had any formal medical training—but she'd seen many, many cases of malaria in her years in Africa. She rummaged in the almost bare cupboards, filled a glass syringe with the antimalarial drug chloroquine (pronounced klor-uh-kween), and gave Mabalo the injection he'd been waiting for. Soon he was making his slow way home, leaning heavily on his wife M'buzu's shoulders.

At first, it seemed as though Sister Beata's injection was working, as it has many times before. But after a day or two, Mabalo's fever returned with a vengeance. Soon he was too weak to get up, and his body was ravaged by terrible bouts of diarrhea and uncontrollable vomiting. His wife and two oldest daughters struggled to care for him. Relatives and neighbors took in the six younger children as the crisis in the Lokela hut deepened. Finally, in desperation, M'buzu begged the nuns to visit her husband, hoping they might be able to cure him.

When the sisters entered the family's small hut, they found Mabalo lying on a low bed covered with raffia matting, bathed in sweat and gasping for breath. Buzzing flies were gathering on patches of dark blood spreading from his ears and pooling beneath his nose and eyes. As they stared, terrified by the change that had come over him, Mabalo convulsed and vomited a stream of blackish blood.

M'buzu turned to the frightened nun beside her. "Sister, can you help? Do you have any medicine that will cure him?"

Slowly, Sister Beata shook her head. "This is new," she said quietly. "This is definitely new."

No one realized it, but the virus that had infected Mabalo was causing his internal organs to disintegrate into a soupy mess, which was seeping from his orifices and through his skin. With every retch, Mabalo released millions of infectious microbes into his surroundings. Every blood- and vomit-soaked rag his daughters washed was a time bomb of lethal micro-organisms. Sister Beata was right: this disease was new, and it was incredibly dangerous.

HELP US!

For seven long days and nights, the nuns and M'buzu fought to keep Mabalo alive. But at last he was claimed by the nightmarish illness.

Surrounded by her children, and helped by her family members and neighbors, M'buzu began preparing her husband's body for the funeral. Together, the group carefully washed the body, sponging away the thick-crusted blood. They would sit with the body all day and all night before carrying Mabola to the prepared grave just outside the family's hut.

As the wails of mourners reverberated through the hot, still air, the nuns, gathered in prayer in the mission's tiny church, felt a sense of relief. Mabalo's illness, as terrifying as it had been, was now over. Life could return to normal in the village and the mission.

But a few days later, everyone began getting sick.

Mabalo's wife, his eldest daughter, his mother, his sister, and his mother-in-law were among the first to come to the mission clinic suffering from fever, headache, vomiting, and diarrhea. More followed. Within days, 21 people who had attended Mabalo's funeral were showing symptoms of the same violent illness. Others in the village, and throughout the surrounding area, were falling ill as well.

The nuns, with their limited knowledge of medical procedures and scanty supplies, struggled to comfort the dying. Then they too began dying. Sister Beata was among the first.

In the mission office, Sister Marcella, the Mother Superior, hunched over the shortwave radio sending message after message to the outside world, pleading for help. The fever was spreading fast, and it killed almost every person it touched, young or old, healthy or frail.

HELP!

For the nuns, for the grieving families, for the villagers numb with fear, there were so many questions. What was causing this terrible disease? Why had it chosen to strike their village? How was it being it spread, and how could the living protect themselves from this killer?

A MICROSCOPIC QUESTION MARK

As the first of October dawned in Yambuku, the epidemic was in its third week. Already well over 100 people were dead. Alerted by Sister Marcella's calls for help, doctors from Zaire's capital city, Kinshasa, arrived by helicopter, collected blood samples, then fled back to safety outside the epidemic zone.

Sister Marcella ordered the mission's gates chained shut, and the remaining patients sent home. There were no longer enough living staff to care for the sick and dying. The remaining nuns gathered together in the mission chapel, praying and waiting for death.

With no clinic to care for the sick, fever patients were taken to neighboring villages to be cared for by family members—spreading the infection throughout the region. Village elders warned people to stay home. Schools and shops closed, social gatherings were discouraged, and trees were felled to block the roads. Almost overnight, the epidemic zone became a network of ghost towns.

But help was on the way. The samples the Kinshasa doctors had collected were winging their way around the globe. In labs across Europe and North America, scientists were peering into microscopes and realizing with a jolt of fear and excitement that they were looking at a virus that had never been seen before.

In Belgium, 27-year-old Dr. Peter Piot, a researcher in the microbiology lab at the Prince Leopold Institute of Tropical Medicine, was one of the first to look down the barrel of a microscope at the virus. He learned quickly that the mysterious microbes were lethal: laboratory mice injected with just tiny amounts died within days. Doctors in Zaire had suspected the disease might be related to yellow fever, but all the antibody tests were coming up negative. With its curved, whiplike tail, the virus looked to Piot like a question mark—a question mark taunting him and his colleagues.

When the director of the institute told Piot that the World Health Organization (WHO) was sending an international team of scientists to Zaire, Piot didn't ask to go—he demanded to be sent as Belgium's representative. This deadly virus was a question to which he was determined to find the answers.

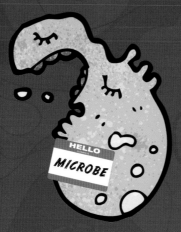

MEET THE MICROBE

"Watch out, I've got a nasty virus. You don't want to catch it."

We've all heard that before. But what exactly are viruses?

A virus is a type of microbe, or single-celled organism. Microbes are the oldest and most numerous life form on earth, and they are essential to human life.

Without microbes we couldn't digest our food, breathe, break down wastes, or do a range of other tasks vital to our survival. But despite being useful in so many ways, microbes have a bad reputation. That's because, amidst the vast diversity of microbes, there are some that cause disease—and in the case of viruses like Ebola, potentially lethal disease.

Viruses are the tiniest, and in many ways the strangest, of all the types of microbes. Scientists can't even agree on whether viruses are alive, strictly speaking. Until a virus comes into contact with a host cell, it is nothing more than a lifeless bundle of DNA. But once it makes contact with cells in your body, the virus springs to life, hijacking the cells and using them to reproduce itself and spread. Illnesses from the common cold to AIDS and Ebola are all caused by viruses. And many of the symptoms of viral illnesses—such as coughing, vomiting, and diarrhea—help to spread the virus to new hosts.

ON THE HUNT

Days later, sitting on a flight to Kinshasa, Dr. Piot started to wonder what he'd gotten himself into. His seatmate, a powerful Belgian diplomat to Zaire, was incensed to learn why the young doctor was on his way to Africa: "Intolerable! We're facing a terrible epidemic, and all they could find is you? How old are you? Twenty-seven? You're totally green, you're barely even a doctor. You've never seen Africa in your life!"

The taxi ride through Kinshasa didn't help to calm Piot's growing nervousness. Everywhere he looked there were throngs of people, and the sticky heat and humidity had him panting. Chaotic traffic jammed the litter-choked streets. He'd hardly been out of Belgium before, and never anywhere as unfamiliar as this city. Had he been foolish to sign up for this mission?

The hastily assembled group of scientists knew only one thing for sure: they didn't have enough information. They needed a scouting team to head for Yambuku, the center of the epidemic, and report back on the scale of the disaster, the conditions in the affected region, and, if possible, the source of the infection and how it was spread. The team would have just four days to collect enough information so a full-scale epidemiological investigation could move in. Who was willing to volunteer?

Before the question was even finished, Piot had his hand up.

COLLECTING CLUES

"*Yaaaa!*" Piot gasped and choked, his throat searing with pain. Around him, a circle of men laughed uproariously. As soon as his eyes stopped watering, Piot joined in the laughter.

It was his first taste of arak, a powerful homemade alcohol popular among Zairean villagers. As Piot was discovering, sharing a drink of the fiery liquor with the community leaders was an important part of gathering information about the epidemic.

He had arrived early that morning in Yalikonde, the nearest village to Yambuku. As he stepped from the Jeep, he was struck by the brooding silence. No children played in the central square, no adults lingered to gossip outside the huts, no shops were open. Only gradually did people emerge from their homes to talk to the foreign doctor.

Later, as the cup of arak was passed from man to man, the village elders revealed how many in the village had died and when. They brought Piot into the huts of the sick, where for the first time he saw the suffering the disease inflicted on its victims. As frightened as he was, Piot felt useful in a way he never had while working in the lab in Belgium. He took blood samples and interviewed family members, noting down everything—the names of the dead, when they had died, their relationships with other fever victims.

The scene in the village square in Yalikonde would be repeated in 10 more villages that day, and in more than 40 others in the days to come. By visiting every village within driving distance of Yambuku, the scouting team determined that over 200 fever deaths had occurred so far, and there were still infected victims.

FROM SOCCER TO FUNERALS

Each night when the WHO team members returned to their headquarters at the Yambuku mission, they shared the data they had collected and the notes they had taken. Soon the scientists had enough information to plot graphs of the disease, showing the number of cases by location, age, and gender, and the dates of known deaths. To everyone's relief, the graphs indicated that the worst of the epidemic was probably already over.

The scouting team was doing its job: collecting enough information so that a full-scale investigation could be set up in the region. But Peter Piot was frustrated. He wanted to find answers to the questions that were tormenting him. How was the disease being transmitted? Why had it spread so quickly from Mabalo Lokela to the rest of the village? And where had the virus come from?

One evening Piot drove to a nearby village, Yamotili-Moke. The village elders welcomed him, and soon a lively debate began about the strengths and weaknesses of Belgian and African soccer players. Peter stayed and talked through the evening, and he returned again the following night. Unlike the systematic data-gathering he did during the day, during these conversations Piot took no notes. He just listened, piecing together information about local customs and culture. He wasn't sure how this would help to fight the epidemic, but he knew that if he wanted to help these people, he needed to understand them better.

Piot's instinct soon proved right. One evening the conversation turned to the preparations for the latest fever victim's funeral, and as the men spoke, Piot learned why a pattern of new infections

QUALITATIVE RESEARCH

When Peter Piot arrived in Zaire, he had no formal training as an epidemiologist. Very few people at that time did. Aside from a few internationally recognized organizations, such as the U.S. Center for Disease Control in Atlanta, Georgia, there were hardly any research laboratories in 1976 that specialized in epidemiology. That meant scientists learned epidemiology on the job.

Piot's team in Zaire took blood samples, drew detailed maps of epidemic-stricken areas, asked the same questions of people over and over again, and noted down everything. But Piot realized that in addition to the "how many" approach of quantitative research (for example, finding out how many people had come into contact with each patient, and how many of those people got sick), the researchers needed to add the element of "why." They needed a "why" approach. Why were some people getting infected when others weren't? To find the answer, they needed to spend time with the villagers, learning the details of their everyday lives. This kind of approach is called qualitative research.

followed each funeral. The custom was for family members of the deceased to wash the body by hand and then to hold a vigil over the body before burial. These practices meant that there were many opportunities to come into contact with infected blood and body fluids. Piot immediately advised the elders to put a stop to their customary funeral rituals for fever victims.

In reviewing the data the team had collected, Piot had noticed something else that worried him. The numbers of young women contracting the disease were abnormally high. Usually in an

NAME THAT VIRUS

If a doctor suspects that you have a virus, you may be asked to provide a sample of your blood to send to a lab, to confirm the diagnosis and identify what the virus is. But what exactly happens in the lab? How do the laboratory scientists determine what's making you sick?

Laboratory scientists today can choose from a few different methods of identifying a virus. One of the oldest methods, developed in the early 1900s, is to grow a "culture" of the virus. To do so, the scientist places a small sample of the infected blood or tissue in a cup, along with cells in which the virus can grow— the culture. As the virus grows in the culture, changes in the cells will be visible under a microscope. By observing these changes, the scientist can identify the virus.

In 1890, German scientist Robert Koch suggested four guidelines for scientists to follow, to help them determine if an infectious organism (such as a virus) is the cause of a specific disease. These rules, still followed by scientists today, are now called "Koch's Postulates." According to these rules, a scientist must be able to answer "yes" to each of the following questions before concluding that a virus causes a particular disease:

1 Is the organism found in people with the disease and absent in people without the disease?

2 Can the organism be grown from blood or tissue samples taken from a person sick with the disease?

3 When the organism is given to a healthy person, do they develop the disease?

4 Can the organism be grown again, from blood or tissue samples from this second person?

epidemic, more deaths were to be expected among the elderly or the very young—those without reserves of strength to fight the disease. But in this case, it looked as though those most vulnerable were women between 18 and 25. The number of deaths of young women was more than double that of young men. What could be the explanation?

Piot recalled what he'd learned about the activities at the Yambuku mission clinic before the epidemic had forced it to close. Despite a tiny staff and only the most basic equipment and supplies, the mission had served the medical needs of thousands of people throughout the region, including offering prenatal care for pregnant women. Piot was willing to bet that many of those expectant mothers were between the ages of 18 and 25.

Could there be a connection between the mission and this terrible epidemic?

Piot knew he needed to get a look at the clinic for himself.

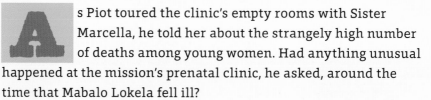

CRACKING THE CASE

As Piot toured the clinic's empty rooms with Sister Marcella, he told her about the strangely high number of deaths among young women. Had anything unusual happened at the mission's prenatal clinic, he asked, around the time that Mabalo Lokela fell ill?

Sister Marcella smiled as she remembered those happier days, when the mission's courtyards had been filled with the bustle of patients and families. She told Piot proudly about the excellent pre-natal care that young mothers received at the clinic, and in particular the popular weekly vitamin shots. All pregnant women visiting the mission clinic were given an injection of vitamin B12.

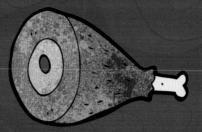

WHERE DOES EBOLA COME FROM?

Peter Piot's team never learned how Mabalo Lokela contracted Ebola, but we now know it is transmitted to humans through contact with infected animals. The Ebola virus has been identified in gorillas and chimpanzees in Africa, and scientists think that in at least some outbreaks, the index case—Patient Zero—was either a local hunter or a customer who bought infected meat from hunters.

Gorillas aren't the reservoir species for the virus (where the virus lives in between the human outbreaks), because Ebola kills gorillas almost as fast as it kills humans. Although it has yet to be proven conclusively, evidence currently points to African fruit bats as the reservoir species. Fruit bats may infect humans directly or transmit the virus to them indirectly, through other animals.

The key to preventing future outbreaks of Ebola is reducing the risk of animal-to-human transmission, particularly from eating wild meat. That may sound simple, but it isn't. Here are some of the reasons that Ebola outbreaks are likely to keep happening in Africa:

- **disappearing forests:** logging and farming are putting more people into formerly wild areas, and into contact with animals

- **war:** refugees fleeing from wars often depend on wild meat for food

- **climate change:** habitats are changing, and some animals are moving closer to human settlements

- **poverty:** there aren't enough hospitals or doctors in some areas of Africa

With a growing sense of dread, Piot asked to see the clinic's dispensary, where all the drugs and medical equipment were stored. In that small bare room, he opened drawers and cupboards one after another. Finally, he turned to Sister Marcella.

"There are only five syringes here for the entire clinic. How did you manage to give so many injections with such a small stock?"

The sister replied matter-of-factly that each morning the syringes were sterilized. After that, they were used over and over again for all the patients treated that day, with a quick rinse between uses. On their meager budget, she explained, the clinic couldn't afford to buy more syringes or needles.

Piot realized with horror that the nun who had given Mabalo Lokela his shot of chloroquine had unwittingly spread the infection to every pregnant woman in the village through the unsterilized needle. Here was the link he'd been searching for. The epidemic had been spread by the very clinic to which people had turned for help.

Piot carefully bagged two of the syringes to take back to Kinshasa for testing. "I'd bet anything these are both infected," he thought sadly to himself.

The conclusions that the scouting team reached were proven correct: the epidemic had spread through unsterilized needles and through contact with infected patients in the mission clinic and at funerals. The last infected patient died on November 5, and there were no further cases reported. The international scientific delegation continued to work in Zaire for several months, collecting as much information as they could about the mysterious disease that they began to call Ebola, after a nearby river.

HOT LABS

Microbiology laboratories around the world use a numbering system to identify their level of biosafety. There are four levels. In Level 1 labs, scientists work only with organisms that do not cause disease. In Level 2 labs, mild disease-causing microbes can be handled. Level 3 labs work with serious diseases for which treatments or vaccines exist. Only in Level 4 labs are the most lethal, highly infectious, and untreatable diseases allowed.

To get clearance to study life-threatening microbes, Level 4 labs must create hot zones: isolation chambers located either in a separate building or in a highly controlled area within the main lab. Before entering a hot zone, researchers dress in special coveralls, over which they pull a bright blue, heavy-duty pressurized hazmat (hazardous materials) suit equipped with a breathing apparatus called a Chemturion. Before entering and after leaving the hot zone, the researcher must also pass through a series of decontamination showers, a vacuum room, and an ultraviolet light room, in order to eliminate all potential traces of disease.

There are 50 of these Level 4 labs across the globe—15 of them are in the U.S., and there is 1 in Canada: the National Microbiology Lab in Winnipeg, Manitoba. It was there, in the summer of 2012, that scientists developed the first potential treatment for Ebola: a drug cocktail that is effective in treating the disease in monkeys.

THE ROAD AHEAD

Researchers eventually identified the Ebola virus as a filovirus—one of only two ever discovered. The filoviruses are a small family of viruses causing extremely lethal diseases in humans. Both filoviruses, Ebola and Marburg, cause severe hemorrhagic (pronounced hem-or-rhag-ik) fever—illnesses in which the victims bleed profusely. Ebola kills 88 percent of its victims, making it one of the most lethal diseases on the planet. In the Yambuku outbreak, 318 people were infected, and 280 died.

Since the epidemic in Yambuku, there have been a number of other Ebola outbreaks in Africa and around the world. Between 1977 and 2012, 29 outbreaks occurred, and 3 of them were in the United States. The Ebola outbreaks in the U.S. happened in research facilities in Virginia and Texas, and the disease was spread from monkeys that had recently been imported from the Philippines. Four workers were accidentally bitten by the monkeys, and tests afterward showed that they had Ebola antibodies in their blood— proteins produced by their immune systems in response to the Ebola virus. But the workers never developed symptoms, although the monkeys became sick with Ebola and most died. This particular strain of Ebola, which is not dangerous to humans, was named Ebola-Reston, after the city in Virginia where it was first identified.

While the actual number of deaths to date from Ebola is small, at roughly 1,500, the impact of Ebola on the public imagination has been enormous. At the time Ebola emerged in 1976, medical science had seemed to be winning the war against disease, with powerful weapons like vaccines and antibiotics in its arsenal. But Ebola reminded everyone of the vast number and diversity of disease-causing viruses and bacteria, and of how much scientists and doctors still had to learn about fighting disease.

In addition, for the first time people realized that modern transportation had the potential to spread viruses around the globe with incredible speed and efficiency. The time it takes to fly between Kinshasa and any major city in North America or Europe is much less than the incubation period for Ebola. Medical care in the Democratic Republic of the Congo is still very basic for most people, because years of civil war in that country have left the population very poor, and roads, hospitals, and medical clinics are in bad repair or have been destroyed. That makes the possible re-emergence of Ebola in that country an ongoing concern, and one that international health organizations take very seriously.

ZOMBIES!

Watched any good movies lately? Did you see the one where an epidemic threatens to destroy life on earth? There's a lot to choose from—movies about mysterious, scary infections are very popular. Especially when they turn people into zombies! Some people argue that the fascination with zombies started with Ebola. While zombies (or the idea of them) have been around in folklore for hundreds of years, they may be so popular today because diseases like Ebola have us worried about infections that spread like lightning—like a zombie apocalypse.

CAREFUL!
THERE'S NO CURE

More than 30 years after the first outbreak, we still don't have an effective treatment or vaccine for Ebola. Doctors and nurses run a high risk of contracting and spreading the disease if they accidentally come into contact with a patient's infected bodily fluids. Poor hygiene practices in rural medical clinics have helped spread many of the Ebola epidemics over the past 30 years.

The World Health Organization recommends that suspected Ebola patients be treated using barrier nursing techniques, which means that patients must be kept in strict isolation, and all medical staff must wear protective gear and take extreme precautions to make sure that no contact with bodily fluids occurs. Patients who die from Ebola must be buried promptly, and there should be no direct contact with the body.

Even when patients recover from Ebola, those around them need to continue taking precautions to make sure they don't become infected. Tests have shown that the virus can linger in the bodily fluids of recovered patients for up to six weeks.

7

A MODERN PLAGUE

AIDS IN THE U.S., 1980

Michael sighed and shifted in his seat, searching for a comfortable position. He crossed his legs, uncrossed them, turned, twisted, slumped so his head rested on the seat back—then straightened up again irritably. It was just no good. He'd been sitting on this hard plastic bench, in this stuffy room, for hours. He felt terrible, and he was pretty sure that at this rate he was going to be spending his whole night here, in the emergency waiting room of the Los Angeles Hospital.

He looked around. Since he'd first walked in, the faces in the waiting room had hardly changed. There was the old Chinese man with the rattling cough, over in the corner was the anxious couple with the crying baby, next to them was the young black man holding the bloody bandage around his hand, and two seats down was that angry woman, rocking and muttering to herself. All of them looked tired and gray-faced—not at all the glamorous jet-setters he'd imagined himself among when he made the big move to Los Angeles a few years ago.

Feeling lost and alone, Michael wondered if he'd done the right thing by moving to L.A. Did he really belong here, in this big faceless city? Back in his hometown, whenever he got sick, he could drop by his family doctor's and count on getting a thorough checkup right away.

Michael reminded himself that he'd come to L.A. for good reasons. Number one, he'd always dreamed of making it big as a model, and that wasn't going to happen in his small hometown. And number two, he was gay. He wanted to live where he could be himself, not hiding or masking his true feelings.

In 1980, being a gay man was tough—there weren't that many places where you could count on a community of people to support you. In L.A. he'd found that community, other young gay men like himself, who'd come to the big city from small towns across the U.S. They'd all taken big risks. Many had left behind families and friends who didn't understand or accept them. He'd formed close friendships in L.A. and built a new life for himself.

"Michael? Is there a Michael here?"

Michael shook himself out of his stupor, realizing with a jolt that the bored and weary nurse with the clipboard was actually calling his name. "Yes! Yes, I'm coming."

He struggled up out of the plastic seat, dismayed at how weak and dizzy he felt. The nurse flicked open a curtain and ushered him into the first cubicle, motioning for him to sit up on the edge of the high hospital bed. When he'd seated himself, she rattled back the curtain and vanished, the words "Doctor'll be here soon" coming faintly through the thin green drape.

Michael prepared himself for another epic wait. But it wasn't long before the curtain swept open again, revealing a white-coated medical resident—a doctor in training. The resident listened closely as Michael described his symptoms, scribbling notes and nodding. The sore throat, for weeks now; the difficulty swallowing; the weakness and fatigue; the fevers; the weight he couldn't stop losing. Michael joked ruefully, "I'm so skinny now, I can't even get modeling jobs. Too thin to model—that's got to be a first!"

The resident paused in his note-taking to study his patient, taking in the chiseled cheekbones, the bright blue eyes and short blond hair. He also noticed Michael's gaunt arms and legs, the deep shadows under his eyes, his labored breathing—all signs pointing to how sick this young man was. The resident pursed his lips.

"If you don't mind waiting some more, I'd like to call in a colleague on your case. An expert. We may need to run some tests."

A PUZZLING SITUATION

 omewhere on Dr. Michael Gottlieb's desk the phone was ringing. But where?

Gottlieb scrabbled frantically through the piles of paper—research reports, medical files, lecture notes—until his hand encountered the receiver. He grabbed it and pulled it up through the layers, yelling, "Hello, hello! Gottlieb here!" before it even got close to his face.

Michael Gottlieb had been working as an assistant professor of immunology at the University of California at Los Angeles Hospital for four months now. He still hadn't managed to get his filing system properly set up, but he had convinced his residents and students to keep their eyes open for patients who showed symptoms of uncommon diseases. So when his phone rang late that December evening in 1980, he guessed that it might be a report of an interesting new case he could use to teach medical students about immunology—the study of the body's systems for fighting disease.

What he heard from the resident on the other end of the phone soon had him running down to the emergency room.

When Dr. Gottlieb examined Michael, he discovered that his sore throat was the result of a severe case of thrush. Thrush is an infection of the mouth, throat, and tongue, caused when the fungus *Candida albicans* accumulates on their surfaces. Dr. Gottlieb wouldn't have been surprised to see thrush in a young baby with an immature immune system, or in a cancer patient whose immune system had been weakened by chemotherapy drugs. But why would Michael get thrush? He was an apparently healthy young man, with no history of immune system problems. And what about his weight loss? Was that connected to this mysterious infection somehow?

Dr. Gottlieb was intrigued—and worried. His apprehension grew as Michael outlined how he'd been feeling exhausted for weeks and was troubled by unexplained fevers. Gottlieb decided to admit Michael to the hospital for a few days while he searched for the cause of his illnesses.

As Dr. Gottlieb would remember afterward, "It was just such a striking, dramatic illness, and he was so critically ill. It was a distinctly unusual thing for someone previously healthy to walk into a hospital so significantly ill. It just didn't fit any recognized disease or syndrome that we were aware of."

For a first step, Dr. Gottlieb decided to give Michael a blood test. When the results of that test landed on his desk, he decided to go talk to Michael.

Michael was in bed, looking even thinner and paler than he had just a few nights earlier in the emergency room when Gottlieb had first met him. The doctor sat down beside the bed and tried to smile, disguising the alarm he felt. "Michael, we've found something kind of unusual. You've got a very low white blood cell count. Do you know what that means?"

Michael looked steadily back at the intense young doctor and tried to joke: "No white blood cells, huh? Well, I guess that must mean that I'm a 100 percent red-blooded American male."

Gottlieb laughed appreciatively. "Oh, sure. Definitely. But here's the thing, Michael. If we think of your body as an army, then the white blood cells are the advance troops, sent out to detect and take down enemy invaders. They defend you against infections. Without white blood cells, your immune system can't do its job. That's why you've got this bad case of thrush—your body isn't defending itself the way we'd expect. And until we can figure out why your immune system is having so much trouble, you're at risk of getting more infections."

Michael nodded, staring down at the sheets as Gottlieb spoke.

"Your case is a bit of a puzzle so far," the doctor continued. "But I like puzzles, and I'm going to solve this one."

BAD NEWS

D r. Gottlieb prescribed antibiotics to clear up the thrush, and Michael was discharged from the hospital and sent home to recuperate. But a few weeks later, he was back in the emergency room, even sicker than before.

As Gottlieb had predicted, a new infection had slipped past Michael's weakened immune system—and the doctors suspected he now had pneumonia.

Michael lay motionless, too weak to do much more than listen, as the doctor delivered the bad news.

"Michael, you've got a kind of pneumonia called *Pneumocystis carinii*. It's pretty rare, and you've also got another infection, a cytomegalovirus, or CMV, infection. That's what's making you so tired and weak. Both of these are what we call opportunistic infections— viruses that aren't normally a threat to healthy people. They've attacked you because your immune system is so weak right now.

"And," the young doctor confessed, "we still can't figure out why."

A PATTERN EMERGES

Only a few weeks later, Michael died. Gottlieb was no closer to solving the puzzle, but he was determined to keep looking for answers.

Meanwhile, across town, another doctor had a patient with a list of symptoms that didn't make sense. Dr. Joel Weisman was gay, and so were many of the patients who came to see him at his North Hollywood office. One patient, a young gay man, had recently come to Weisman complaining that he was tired all the time, had swollen lymph glands, kept getting fevers, and was losing weight—more than 14 kg (30 pounds) in just a couple of months. The man was getting sicker by the day, but Weisman couldn't figure out why. He decided to refer the case to an immunologist, and he called up Michael Gottlieb.

As Gottlieb listened to Dr. Weisman describe the patient, he had only one thought: "Michael!"

Gottlieb ran blood tests on this new young man, and sure enough, this patient had a CMV infection and hardly any white blood cells. Soon, just like Michael, the young man developed *Pneumocystis carinii*. Not long after, he died.

Could two deaths from such similar causes be simply a strange coincidence? Gottlieb didn't think so, and his hunch was right: three weeks later, he learned that a third patient with the same symptoms had been admitted to hospital in L.A. This case was a replica of the first two: a CMV infection, a low white blood cell count, a lung infection. Clearly, a pattern was emerging. All three men were young and healthy, but had severely damaged immune systems. All three of the men were also homosexual. Gottlieb and Weisman were worried. What was making these young men so sick? Whatever it was, it was lethal.

Gottlieb started calling around to other hospitals and doctors in California, asking if they had seen any cases of CMV infection or pneumocystis recently. A hospital in Santa Barbara had, and they sent him their records on the case. When Gottlieb read that the patient in Santa Barbara was gay, he knew that puzzle pieces were starting to fall into place.

He decided to get in touch with an old friend from medical school. Dr. Wayne Shandera was L.A.'s epidemic control officer, part of the Epidemiology Intelligence Service. Shandera had trained at the Center for Disease Control in Atlanta, and now he was L.A.'s chief disease watcher.

Gottlieb told Shandera what had been happening in the past few weeks. Shandera hadn't heard of anything that could be making young men in L.A. sick, and he felt the deaths might be just coincidental. But the next day, a report landed on his desk about a man from Santa Monica, near L.A., who had been diagnosed with pneumocystis pneumonia. Shandera decided to take a drive down there.

At the hospital in Santa Monica, Shandera discovered that the patient was 29 years old, with no history of immune system problems, and that he was gay. When further tests showed that the patient also had a CMV infection, Shandera called his friend Michael Gottlieb and told him that he had just found a fifth case.

As Gottlieb later recalled, "A shiver went down my spine. With just a little bit of information, [Shandera] was able to go right out and find a case." The two doctors suspected they were seeing the beginnings of an epidemic. But was it just in their region? Or could it be happening elsewhere in the country too?

To find out, they needed to let other doctors know about the cases in L.A. In June 1981 they wrote a brief article about Michael and the other patients they'd encountered, which was published in *The Morbidity and Mortality Weekly Report—MMWR*, as it's known among doctors—a medical journal from the U.S. Centers for Disease Control.

Soon, the phones at the CDC's headquarters in Atlanta started ringing with calls from doctors in New York, New Jersey, and San Francisco. Within a month, the CDC knew of 15 young men around the country who had developed pneumocystis. They'd also heard about 26 cases of young men with Kaposi's sarcoma, a rare form of skin cancer, who also showed depressed immune systems. All the patients were gay.

Over the summer and fall of 1981, doctors at the CDC kept hearing about men struggling with unexplained weight loss, rare forms of tuberculosis, unusual cancers. In New York, San Francisco, and other cities with large gay communities, people were starting to panic, as rumors spread about the deadly new disease some people were calling "gay cancer."

Doctors were frightened too, and helpless to save people. Dr. Donna Mildvan remembers desperately trying to treat a 33-year-old man dying from Kaposi's sarcoma in the summer of 1981: "We tried a few drugs but nothing changed. You *don't* lose a 33-year-old patient. We were agonized."

EPIDEMIC INTELLIGENCE SERVICE

When Dr. Wayne Shandera wrote the article describing the first five cases of what would later be called AIDS, he was still in training—as a "disease detective." Shandera was in L.A. because he had been accepted into the Epidemic Intelligence Service (EIS), a two-year training program still run today by the U.S. Centers for Disease Control that turns doctors and other medical and scientific professionals into highly skilled medical detectives. The EIS is intended to be the medical equivalent of the Central Intelligence Agency, or CIA—but the enemies the EIS agents hunt down are biological.

Every year, 80 of the top medical and scientific graduates in the U.S. are accepted into the EIS program. For two years, they are on 24-hour alert, and they have to be ready at a moment's notice to travel to the latest epidemic hotspot. The logo of the EIS features a shoe with a hole in it, over a map of the world. It's a reference to the "shoe-leather epidemiology" pioneered by John Snow, and it's the way these epidemiologists still work: going from door to door in the middle of an epidemic to get the information they need to stop the outbreak. The EIS officers don't just travel by foot, though—they'll do whatever it takes to get where they need to go, whether that means going by helicopter, dugout canoe, dogsled, camel, or even elephant.

Today, there are programs like the Epidemic Intelligence Service in 36 countries, with more in development. Besides being at the forefront of the identification of AIDS, epidemiologists with the EIS identified Legionnaires' disease, helped to eradicate smallpox, developed effective treatments for cholera, and proved that Lyme disease comes from ticks, among many other important achievements.

Epidemiologists at the CDC had no idea how the disease was spreading. Was it sexually transmitted? Did it come from food, or from a drug? Was it contagious, like a cold or the flu? No one knew, and people kept dying.

SOLVING THE PUZZLE

All the patients who had been seen so far were gay men. But not all gay men were getting sick. So, what was the determining factor? To find out, researchers at the CDC decided to perform case control studies, which would compare patients to "controls"—healthy individuals who shared many characteristics with the patients. In Los Angeles, New York, and San Francisco, 180 gay men agreed to take part. Researchers probed into the men's daily lives, health, and backgrounds, looking for clues to what was making some of them sick while others remained healthy.

But even before the studies were completed, it became clear it was not only gay men getting sick with the new disease. The CDC began hearing reports of other patients with depressed immune systems and opportunistic infections. Hemophiliacs were one new group of patients. Hemophilia (pronounced heem-o-fill-ee-ah) is a rare condition in which the blood doesn't clot. People with hemophilia may bleed uncontrollably from even small cuts and scratches, so they often require blood transfusions and blood products that help their blood clot normally. Other new patients included people who used illegal drugs they injected into their veins, like heroin. Doctors knew these drug users often shared needles, which could explain how the disease was spreading among this group.

CALLING FOR CHANGE

Today, gay people in many parts of the world—including Canada, some European countries, and parts of the U.S.—are able to get married, have children, and raise families just like anyone else. So it can be hard to imagine just how different things were 30 or 40 years ago. In the late 1970s and early 1980s, gay people faced lots of discrimination.

In some U.S. states at the time, there were laws against homosexuality, and many gay people remained "in the closet," afraid to let their families and communities know about that part of their lives.

But things were starting to change. In 1979, 100,000 gay men and women marched in Washington, D.C., in the first ever National March for Lesbian and Gay Rights. Large gay communities developed in places like San Francisco, New York, and Los Angeles, as people from around the country came to the cities in search of the freedom to live openly. Governments began passing laws to outlaw discrimination on the basis of sexual orientation.

Attitudes changed more slowly than laws, however, and when AIDS appeared, fear of the deadly disease increased the stigma against gay people. Because of the danger of AIDS, more and more gay people in North America and other parts of the world started to stand up for their rights and to call on governments for action in the fight against the disease. Without the activism of many committed gay and lesbian people, public education campaigns about AIDS might not have happened, research might not have been funded, and many more people would have died.

The evidence was pointing toward a virus transmitted between people through bodily fluids—blood and semen. The researchers at the CDC realized that it was a disease with the potential to go global: anyone could become infected. And doctors still had no way to treat it.

THE EPIDEMIC WITH NO NAME

By the end of 1981, 270 cases of this new disease had been identified in the United States, and 121 of the patients had died. Early in 1982, the disease began to be reported in a number of European countries. And in Africa, doctors in the country of Uganda made a connection between the reports from the U.S. and patients they were seeing who were suffering from an illness known locally as "slim." Slim was a fatal disease that caused severe weight loss, infections, and unusual cancers. It didn't take long to figure out that slim and the "gay cancer" from the U.S. were one and the same. The new disease, doctors began to realize, was already a massive global epidemic.

Unless you were a doctor or a gay man living in the U.S., though, you probably didn't even know that a terrifying new disease was spreading. None of the major TV networks had reported on the story. It wasn't until June 17, 1982, that *NBC Nightly News* featured a story on a "new deadly disease" affecting gay men. And it was almost another year—May 1983—before the *New York Times* newspaper ran a front page article on what was now being called AIDS (acquired immunodeficiency syndrome). By that time the epidemic had been going on for nearly two years, with over 1,400 diagnosed cases in the U.S. More than 500 people had died.

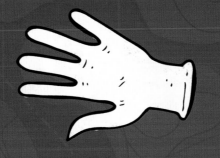

THE STIGMA OF AIDS

In the 1980s, when AIDS was first reported in the media as the "new plague," many people panicked. There were lots of rumors and false information—for example, that you could get AIDS from kissing someone with the disease, or by sharing food with them or drinking from the same glass. Even some medical personnel were afraid to touch AIDS sufferers. Some people were afraid that anyone who was gay might potentially have the disease. And gay men themselves grew terrified as more and more of their friends fell ill. One man from San Francisco remembers that "as the 80s started going along... more and more people were getting sick. Fear was gripping the city and the nation. Gay people stopped going out. Nobody knew how it was transmitted and people were afraid."

Because gay men were the first to get sick, some people argued that AIDS was a punishment, showing that the gay lifestyle was immoral. People who developed AIDS were sometimes shunned, and they were made to feel ashamed for being sick. As the years passed, however, it became clear that AIDS was a disease that everyone—gay or straight, old or young—was vulnerable to, and slowly attitudes began to change. Along with a number of other celebrities, the late Princess Diana of England was credited with helping to change the public's feelings about AIDS patients. During the 1980s and 1990s she was frequently photographed visiting AIDS patients, hugging children with AIDS, and showing that she wasn't afraid of them. Her support for charities that assisted people with AIDS helped to raise the profile of the disease.

The news media in the 1980s may have been uncomfortable reporting on a disease that seemed at first to be confined to gay men and drug users. Or the story may not have seemed important to them. Whatever the reasons, gay activists knew that the story of AIDS needed to be told. They coined the slogan "Silence = Death" to highlight the urgency of making information about AIDS available to the public. In many cities and communities across North America—as well as in England, Australia, and parts of Europe—health activists set up services to help people who'd contracted the disease, offering counseling, free food, and other kinds of day-to-day support.

Scientists in the United States had agreed to call the new disease AIDS. At first, research teams were confident that they would soon be able to develop a vaccine. The search for an AIDS vaccine has been long and difficult—and it's not over yet. In 1987, after years of arguing about who had been the first to discover the virus that causes AIDS, the governments of France and the U.S. agreed to share the discovery, and named the virus HIV, or human immunodeficiency virus. With the virus identified, doctors could begin testing patients' blood, allowing for earlier diagnosis than had been possible before.

Eventually, the government and the media began to respond to the AIDS crisis, especially as it became clear that the epidemic was affecting people from all walks of life. By 1985, more than 6,800 people in the U.S. had died of AIDS. Public health information on AIDS became more widespread, and campaigns to promote safe sex appeared, along with much greater media attention. But the death toll for the AIDS epidemic continued to mount. People who had received blood transfusions were at risk, and many hemophiliacs, including children, developed AIDS. Babies with AIDS were born to mothers who had the virus. With each passing year, the tragedy of AIDS deepened. In 1986 alone there were 12,000 deaths. By 1988 the yearly total had reached 20,000.

By the end of the 1980s, AIDS was on its way to becoming the most devastating epidemic of modern times.

JUST THE FACTS

The terms AIDS and HIV are often used together, but there are some important differences in what they mean. HIV, or human immunodeficiency virus, is the virus that causes AIDS. When a person becomes infected with HIV, the virus attacks their body's white blood cells, reproducing inside each cell and destroying it, then moving on to the next one, until the person's immune system is in tatters. AIDS—acquired immunodeficiency syndrome—is the final stage of HIV infection, when the immune system has become so "deficient" that it can no longer protect the body from infections. At this stage, people begin to suffer from opportunistic infections, such as Kaposi's sarcoma or *Pneumocystis carinii*. Eventually, they die from these illnesses.

Today, people infected with HIV can take anti-retroviral medication to slow down the rate at which the virus reproduces in their bodies. With this therapy, people with HIV/AIDS can avoid opportunistic infections, stay healthy, and live much longer.

AIDS TODAY

Since the beginning of the AIDS pandemic in the 1980s, nearly 70 million people have been infected with the HIV virus. About 35 million people have died of AIDS, according to the World Health Organization. And more than 1.5 million people around the world still die of AIDS each year.

Even more frighteningly, nearly 70 percent of the world's HIV/AIDS patients today are in one area: Africa. In some parts of Africa, about 1 in every 20 adults has HIV. Millions of children have lost their parents to AIDS. Some international organizations predict that by 2020 there will be more than 50 million orphaned children in Africa.

Some of these children are raised by their grandparents. Sometimes the older children in the family are left alone to care for the younger ones. Finding food, clothing, and shelter can be a terrible struggle—and because these children have no opportunity to go to school, their chances of getting out of poverty are very slim. Advocates like Canadian diplomat Stephen Lewis, the former United Nations Special Envoy for HIV/AIDS in Africa, are working with governments and international aid agencies to try to find a solution to the crisis of Africa's orphaned children. It is a huge problem, and solving it will take the efforts of many countries and people around the world working together.

Researchers who study AIDS have many ways to explain why the disease is so much more common in African countries than in other parts of the world. Poverty and lack of education are two very important reasons. Wars and environmental crises in some African countries have also made it very difficult to treat people with HIV and AIDS, and to develop public health programs to prevent the disease.

DISCOVERING THE VIRUS

The virus that causes AIDS was discovered in 1983 by Françoise Barré-Sinoussi, Luc Montagnier, and Jean-Claude Chermann at the Pasteur Institute in Paris, France. The three French scientists took tissue samples from the lymph nodes of AIDS patients. They grew the virus in the laboratory from these samples and identified it using an electron microscope.

A team of American researchers led by Dr. Robert Gallo identified the HIV virus at around the same time, and they claimed to have been the first to make this important discovery. For years the two countries disputed which group of scientists had been first. There was a lot at stake: the American government had registered a patent for an AIDS test based on detecting the presence of HIV, and if it was proven that the French team had discovered the virus first, the money from that patent would go to France.

In 1987 the two countries negotiated a settlement: they would split the proceeds from the patent 50-50. Twenty-one years later, in 2008, the French scientists were awarded the Nobel Prize for medicine for their discovery of HIV.

Today we know that AIDS can only be transmitted through the exchange of bodily fluids, and there are ways to prevent the transmission of AIDS and stay healthy. Practicing safe sex by using condoms during sexual intercourse is one important preventive measure. Not sharing needles is another.

Thanks to education and prevention campaigns in many countries, far fewer people today are becoming infected with HIV. And doctors have developed a number of drugs, collectively called highly active antiretroviral therapy (HAART), that help to bolster immune systems in HIV patients, so that they don't develop opportunistic infections. There is still no vaccine that can prevent HIV/AIDS, though, and retroviral drugs often aren't available to people in poorer countries. That's a situation activists, health-care advocates, and many others worldwide are working hard to change.

Dr. Michael Gottlieb spent the rest of his career working to solve the puzzle of AIDS. He became the chairman of the American Foundation for AIDS Research. But the solution to the puzzle continues to elude scientists, and the AIDS epidemic that killed Michael marches on, spreading to new people around the world every day.

WHO WAS PATIENT ZERO?

In 1987, an American journalist named Randy Shilts published a book entitled *And the Band Played On: Politics, People, and the AIDS Epidemic*. It was an instant bestseller.

The book investigated the reasons it had taken so long in the U.S. for the AIDS epidemic to get attention and funding from government and public health agencies. But what had people really excited was the story Shilts told about one particular man: Gaetan Dugas. Dugas was a French-Canadian flight attendant, and one of the earliest people to get AIDS. He participated in the Centers for Disease Control's case control study, and it turned out that he was the only connection between many of the other patients. He'd infected the others through unprotected sex.

The CDC study identified Dugas only as "Patient 0." However, Shilts discovered his name and publicized him as "the man who spread AIDS from one side of the continent to the other." *Time* magazine ran a story headlined "The Appalling Saga of Patient Zero," and suddenly the AIDS epidemic had a new villain.

Today we know that Gaetan Dugas didn't singlehandedly cause the AIDS epidemic. But in the 1980s, finding someone to blame was one way for people to make sense of this terrifying, unstoppable epidemic. As with Typhoid Mary in the New York outbreaks of typhoid, people saw this Patient Zero as a villain who made others sick through irresponsible behavior.

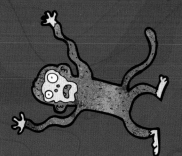

TRACKING DOWN THE SOURCE OF AIDS

In 2006 Dr. Beatrice Hahn, a microbiologist, announced that she and her colleagues at the University of Alabama had discovered the origins of the HIV virus. They had identified a virus that infects wild apes in Africa, called the simian immunodeficiency virus (SIV).

For years, Dr. Hahn had been studying captive chimpanzees. She had previously identified an HIV-like virus in them, but in order to get the scientific community to believe her theory that HIV had come from chimps, she needed to prove that the virus existed in the wild. But how? Turns out the answer was lying on the jungle floor: chimp droppings.

Dr. Hahn and her researchers scoured the jungles of Cameroon and Tanzania, picking up all the fresh chimpanzee poop they could find, and analyzing it. From those fecal samples, they eventually identified SIV.

Hahn believes that at some point an unknown African hunter killed a chimp but cut himself while butchering the animal. The chimp's blood, which was infected with SIV, passed the virus to the hunter. Once inside its new host, the virus mutated, becoming HIV.

The hunter probably lived in a small, isolated village, so at first the virus didn't spread far. But Hahn and her team think that eventually the virus landed in someone traveling south down the Congo River.

"The virus ended up in a major metropolitan area, which would either be Kinshasa or Brazzaville," Dr. Hahn told journalists from *National Geographic* magazine in 2007, naming two cities in the Democratic Republic of the Congo. "That's where we believe the AIDS pandemic really started."

Researchers now think that SIV was passed to humans in the 1930s. A frozen blood sample taken from a man in Kinshasa in 1959 was discovered in 2007 to contain HIV. It is the earliest example of HIV infection. HIV probably reached North America in 1977, but wasn't recognized until the early 1980s.

CONCLUSION

EPIDEMIOLOGY TODAY

A sk Jennifer Gardy why she decided to become an epidemiologist and she smiles mischievously, flicking her bangs out of her eyes. "When I was a kid I saw Dustin Hoffman in the movie *Outbreak*, and I knew right away that's what I wanted to be: a cootie-hunter."

Today Gardy is a doctor, a professor at the University of British Columbia's Faculty of Population Health, and a researcher at the B.C. Centre for Disease Control. She hasn't lost her fascination and wide-eyed enthusiasm for finding new, cool ways of hunting cooties. Lucky visitors at the Centre for Disease Control might just get taken downstairs to peek through the windows into the big basement laboratory where blood and tissue samples from all over the province are analyzed. "Look, look, there it goes! Isn't that cool?" Dr. Gardy whispers, as a robotic arm at one end of a conveyor belt silently slides out to grab a test tube and place it in the open door of a centrifuge. She sounds a bit like a kid on her first amazed visit to a science center—but Dr. Gardy gets to go to this science center every day.

Gardy's specialty is genome sequencing, a cutting-edge technique that looks for tiny changes in the DNA structure of viruses. For instance, by studying the patterns of DNA changes in samples from people in a community who come down with the same strain of flu, Gardy can re-create the path of the outbreak, tracing back to the index case, or Patient Zero.

"Before," she says, "epidemiology involved a lot of guesswork. With genome sequencing, we can know *exactly* where an outbreak started, and how it spread."

Scientists like Gardy hope that one day the data from genome sequencing will be available quickly enough that epidemiologists can use it to stop outbreaks in their initial stages, eventually making epidemics a thing of the past. But as Gardy admits, "Those cooties are clever," and medical science still has a long way to go before it can claim to have conquered disease outbreaks.

As the science of epidemiology becomes more complex, the days of going it alone as a disease detective are coming to an end. That suits Gardy just fine. "I was raised to care and share, not to be a glory-grabber," she says with a smile. Uncovering the mysteries of disease in the 21st century involves doctors, nurses, microbiologists, computer experts, and many other specialists. "We work in teams, because we all have something unique to contribute," Gardy explains.

Today, even Google is helping out in the fight against epidemics. With Google Flu Trends, doctors and public health officials can get an almost "real time" picture of each year's flu epidemic. It's a surprisingly simple way of tracking outbreaks using social media. Traditional flu monitoring comes from national networks of doctors who report cases of patients they've seen with flu. But what do many people do now when they start to feel sick?

They google "flu," "fever," "headache," or "sore throat." While they may not necessarily get good medical advice that way, all those searches provide Google with data about how many people are feeling sick long before doctors find out about it. Google's information may not be as accurate as the conventional method (not everyone who has a fever and a headache has the flu, after all), but it's fast, it can cover a whole region or country, and it can show how an outbreak is spreading.

Google Flu Trends is just one example of how quickly epidemiological tools are changing and evolving, as technology advances. The science of epidemiology has come a long way since John Snow made his map of the Soho cholera outbreak. But there is still a lot of work ahead. "We will always need disease-hunters," Jennifer Gardy says. "Disease is never going to go away." Dr. Gardy and her colleagues around the world—scientists, doctors, researchers, and public health officials—are working hard to make sure that when the next epidemic or pandemic strikes, we're ready to fight back.

GLOSSARY

ANESTHESIA: Any drug given to patients to take away pain during surgery

ANTIBODIES: Substances produced by the immune system to defend the body against viruses or bacteria

BACTERIA (OR BACTERIUM): Single-celled microscopic organism (plural: bacteria)

BUBONIC PLAGUE: Most common form of plague, a severe and sometimes fatal bacterial infection caused by flea bites, with symptoms including swollen lymph nodes (called buboes) and fever

CARRIER: A person infected with a disease who does not have symptoms but can transmit the disease to others

CESSPOOL: Underground chamber containing sewage, usually from a house

CYANOSIS: Reaction of the skin to lack of oxygen, causing it to turn blue

ENDEMIC DISEASE: A disease regularly found in a certain area or population (e.g., chicken pox and mumps are endemic diseases in North America)

EPIDEMIC: A sharp increase in the number of cases of a disease

EPIDEMIOLOGY: The study of diseases, how they spread, and how they can be controlled

FECES: Solid bodily waste

IMMUNOLOGY: Science and study of the immune system, the body's defence against disease

LAUDANUM: Drug derived from opium, formerly used to treat sickness and sedate patients

MIASMA: Vapors formerly thought to contain disease-causing contagion

MORTALITY RATE: Number of deaths in a certain period of time, from a particular cause, in a population (e.g., the mortality rate from car accidents in the U.S. from 1999 to 2005 was 15.4 deaths per 100,000)

MUTATE: To change

PANDEMIC: Global epidemic or series of epidemics of a single disease affecting a large portion of the world at the same time

PNEUMONIC PLAGUE: Disease caused by inhaling infected droplets from another patient, affecting lungs; often fatal

QUALITATIVE RESEARCH: Study of behavior through methods such as observation, interviews, and surveys

QUANTITATIVE RESEARCH: Study of phenomena using statistical techniques and numerical data

QUARANTINE: To keep someone or something apart from others in order to stop the spread of disease; also, the place where people are held while under quarantine

REHYDRATE: To restore lost water to the body (rehydration fluid)

RESERVOIR SPECIES: Organisms that host (or harbor) the microbes that cause a particular disease; usually, the disease does not cause symptoms, or causes only mild symptoms, in the reservoir species (examples are ducks and geese, which are the reservoir species for avian influenza)

SANITATION: Keeping living conditions clean in order to maintain health

SEPTICEMIC PLAGUE: Form of plague in which bacteria invade the bloodstream, causing death

VIRUS: Simplest form of germ, visible only under electron microscope; viruses cause diseases ranging from influenza and the common cold to yellow fever and AIDS

WORKHOUSE: 19th-century institution for housing the poor

WANT TO LEARN MORE?

There are lots of great resources in your local library and online about the history of the diseases described in this book. Check out these suggestions as a starting point for your explorations into the fascinating world of epidemiology:

PLAGUE   *The Great Plague and Fire of London* by Charles J. Shields. Philadelphia, PA: Chelsea House, 2002.
The Plague by Holly Cefrey. New York, NY: Rosen, 2001.

CHOLERA   *The Blue Death: The True Story of a Terrifying Epidemic* by Judy Allen. London, U.K.: Hodder, 2001.
Cholera: Curse of the Nineteenth Century by Stephanie True Peters. New York, NY: Marshall Cavendish, 2005.

TYPHOID   "The Most Dangerous Woman in America." An episode of the *Nova* TV series, PBS, 1996. Go to: www.pbs.org/wgbh/nova/typhoid.
You Wouldn't Want to Meet Typhoid Mary!: A Deadly Cook You'd Rather Not Know by Jacqueline Morley. New York, NY: Franklin Watts/Scholastic Inc., 2013.

YELLOW FEVER   *The Secret of the Yellow Death: A True Story of Medical Sleuthing* by Suzanne Jurmain. Boston, MA: Houghton Mifflin, 2009.

SPANISH INFLUENZA   *The 1918 Influenza Pandemic* by Stephanie True Peters. New York, NY: Marshall Cavendish, 2005.
"Influenza 1918." An episode of the *American Experience* TV series, PBS, 1998. Go to:www.pbs.org/wgbh/americanexperience/features/general-article/influenza-first-wave.

EBOLA   *Ebola* by Aubrey Stimola. New York, NY: Rosen, 2011.
"Ebola—The Plague Fighters." An episode of the *Nova* TV series, PBS, 1996. Go to: www.pbs.org/wgbh/nova/education/programs (select title from the teachers' guides list).
World's Worst Germs: Micro-organisms and Disease by Anna Claybourne. Chicago, IL: Raintree, 2006.

AIDS   *AIDS and HIV: The Facts for Kids* by Rae Simons. Vestal, NY: Alphahouse, 2009.
AIDS: In Search of a Killer by Suzanne Levert. New York, NY: Julian Messner, 1987.
Heroes Against AIDS by Anna Forbes. New York, NY: PowerKids Press, 1996.

SOURCES

CHAPTER 1: London's Dreadful Visitation: The Great Plague Epidemic of 1665

Carmody, John. "John Graunt and the Birth of Medical Statistics." Radio program. *Ockham's Razor.* Australian Broadcasting Corporation. September, 30, 2012. Accessed at: www.abc.net.au/radionational/programs/ockhamsrazor/john-graunt-and-the-birth-of-medical-statistics/4279242#transcript.

Cunningham, Kevin. *Diseases in History: Plague.* Greensboro, NC: Morgan Reynolds Publishing, 2009.

Graunt, John. *Reflections on the weekly bills of mortality for the cities of London and Westminster, and the places adjacent: but more especially, so far as it relates to the plague and other most mortal diseases that we English-men are most subject to, and should be most careful against, in this our age.* London: Printed for Samuel Speed, at the Rainbow in Fleet-Street, 1665. Houghton Library, Harvard University, Cambridge, MA. Accessed at: http://nrs.harvard.edu/urn-3:FHCL.HOUGH:1267760.

Greenberg, S.J. "The Dreadful Visitation: Public Health and Public Awareness in Seventeenth-Century London." *Journal of the Medical Library Association.* October 1997, 85(4): 391–401.

Moote, A. Lloyd, and Dorothy C. Moote. *The Great Plague: The Story of London's Most Deadly Year.* Baltimore, MD: John Hopkins University Press, 2004.

Porter, Stephen. *The Great Plague.* Stroud, U.K.: Sutton Publishing, 1999.

Pryor, E.G. "The Great Plague of Hong Kong." *Journal of the Hong Kong Branch of the Royal Asiatic Society.* Hong Kong: Royal Asiatic Society of Great Britain and Ireland, 1975: 61–70.

Rothman, Kenneth J. "Lessons from John Graunt." *The Lancet*, 1996, 347: 37–39. Accessed at: www.sjsu.edu/faculty/gerstman/eks/RothmanArticleOnGraunt1996.pdf.

Stephan, Ed. "John Graunt (1620–1674)." Web database on Graunt's work. Accessed at www.edstephan.org/Graunt/graunt.html.

CHAPTER 2: Plotting a Mystery: The Soho Cholera Outbreak of 1854

Allen, Judy. *The Blue Death: The True Story of a Terrifying Epidemic.* London, U.K.: Hodder, 2001.

Hempel, Sandra. *The Strange Case of the Broad Street Pump: John Snow and the Mystery of Cholera.* Berkeley, CA: University of California Press, 2007.

Johnson, Steven. *The Ghost Map: The Story of London's Most Terrifying Epidemic— And How It Changed Science, Cities, and the Modern World.* New York, NY: Riverhead Books, 2006.

Muench, Susan Bandoni. *The Mystery of the Blue Death: A Case Study in Epidemiology and the History of Science.* New York, NY: National Center for Case Study Teaching in Science, 2009.

Peters, Stephanie True. *Cholera: Curse of the Nineteenth Century.* New York, NY: Marshall Cavendish, 2005.

Sample, Ian. "Click Clinica: The App That Maps Disease Outbreaks." *The Guardian*, November 26, 2012. Accessed at: www.guardian.co.uk/science/blog/2012/nov/26/clickclinicaapp-map-disease-outbreaks.

CHAPTER 3: "Did the Mosquito Do It?" Yellow Fever in Cuba, 1900

Agramonte, Aristides. *The Inside Story of a Great Medical Discovery*. Havana: Times of Cuba Press, 1915; Seattle, WA: The World Wide School Library, 1998. Accessed at: www.worldwideschool.org/library/books/tech/medicine/YellowFever.

Altman, Lawrence K. *Who Goes First?: The Story of Self-Experimentation in Medicine*. New York, NY: Random House, 1987.

Dickerson, James L. *Yellow Fever: A Deadly Disease Poised to Kill Again*. Amherst, NY: Prometheus Books, 2006.

Jurmain, Suzanne. *The Secret of the Yellow Death: A True Story of Medical Sleuthing*. Boston, MA: Houghton Mifflin, 2009.

McCullough, David. *The Path Between the Seas: The Creation of the Panama Canal, 1870–1914*. New York: Simon and Schuster, 1977.

CHAPTER 4: A Special Guest of the City of New York: Typhoid in 1906

Bourdain, Anthony. *Typhoid Mary: An Urban Historical*. New York, NY: Bloomsbury, 2001.

Leavitt, Judith Walzer. *Typhoid Mary: Captive to the Public's Health*. Boston, MA: Beacon Press, 1996.

Parry, Manon S. "Sara Josephine Baker (1873–1945)." *American Journal of Public Health*, April 2006, 96(4): 620–21.

CHAPTER 5: "Send the Word to Beware": The Spanish Influenza Pandemic, 1918–19

Barry, John M. *The Great Influenza: The Story of the Deadliest Pandemic in History*. New York, NY: Penguin, 2004.

Cohan, George M. "Over There." Audio recording, 1917. Accessed at: www.firstworldwar.com/audio/overthere.htm.

Crosby, Alfred W. *America's Forgotten Pandemic: The Influenza of 1918*. Cambridge, U.K.: Cambridge University Press, 2003.

Daniel, Thomas M. *Wade Hampton Frost, Pioneer Epidemiologist 1880–1938: Up to the Mountain*. Rochester, NY: University of Rochester Press, 2004.

Duncan, Kirsty. *Hunting the 1918 Flu: One Scientist's Search for a Killer Virus*. Toronto, ON: University of Toronto Press, 2003.

Frost, Wade Hampton. "The Epidemiology of Influenza." *Journal of the American Medical Association*. August 1919, 73: 313–18.

Peters, Stephanie True. *The 1918 Influenza Pandemic*. New York, NY: Marshall Cavendish, 2005.

CHAPTER 6: Mystery in the Jungle: Ebola in Zaire, 1976

Close, William T. *Ebola: Through the Eyes of the People*. Marbleton, WY: Meadowlark Springs Productions, 2002.

Garrett, Laurie. *The Coming Plague: Newly Emerging Diseases in a World Out of Balance*. New York, NY: Penguin, 1995.

Garrett, Laurie. "A Conversation with Peter Piot." Transcript, June 18, 2012,

Council on Foreign Relations. Accessed at: www.cfr.org/global-health/conversation-peter-piottranscript/p28710.

Lovgren, Stefan. "Where Does Ebola Hide Between Epidemics?" Article for National Geographic News, February 19, 2003. Accessed at: http://news.national-geographic.com/news/2003/02/0219_030219_ebolaorigin.html.

Piot, Peter. *No Time to Lose: A Life in Pursuit of Deadly Viruses*. New York, NY: W.W. Norton & Co., 2012.

"Robert Koch, 1843–1910." Uncredited webpage. In *Contagion: Historical Views of Diseases and Epidemics*. Harvard University Library Open Collections Program. Accessed at: http://ocp.hul.harvard.edu/contagion/koch.html.

Smith, Tara C. *Ebola*. Deadly Diseases and Epidemics series. New York, NY: Chelsea House Publications, 2005.

Stimola, Aubrey. *Ebola*. New York, NY: Rosen Publishing, 2011.

Sureau, P., P. Piot, et al. "Containment and Surveillance of an Epidemic of Ebola Virus Infection in Yambuku Area, Zaire, 1976." In *Proceedings of an International Colloquium on Ebola Virus Disease and other Haemorrhagic Fevers held in Antwerp, Belgium, 6–8 December, 1977*, ed. S.R. Pattyn. Amsterdam: Elsevier/North Holland Biomedical Press B.V., 1978.

CHAPTER 7: A Modern Plague: AIDS in the U.S., 1980

Brown, David. "The Emergence of a Deadly Disease," *Washington Post*, June 5, 2001. Accessed at: www.washingtonpost.com/wp-dyn/content/article/2006/06/03/AR2006060300452.html.

Epidemic Intelligence Service (EIS) webpages. Centers for Disease Control and Prevention website. Accessed at: www.cdc.gov/EIS/index.html.

Fan, Hung Y., Ross F. Conner, and Luis P. Villarreal. *AIDS: Science and Society*. Burlington, MA: Jones & Bartlett, 2007.

Fisher, Max. "The Story of AIDS in Africa." *The Atlantic*, December 1, 2011. Accessed at: www.theatlantic.com/international/archive/2011/12/the-story-of-aids-in-africa/249361/.

Kinsella, J. *Covering the Plague: AIDS and the American Media*. New Brunswick, NJ: Rutgers University Press, 1989.

Knox, Richard. "Epicenter of AIDS Is Found: Africa, 1930." *All Things Considered* radio program episode, National Public Radio, May 25, 2006. Accessed at: www.npr.org/templates/story/story.php?storyId=5431256.

Levert, Suzanne. *AIDS: In Search of a Killer*. New York, NY: Julian Messner, 1987.

Owen, James. "AIDS Origin Traced to Chimp Group in Cameroon." Article for National Geographic News, May 26, 2006. Accessed at: http://news.nationalgeo-graphic.com/news/2006/05/060525-aids-chimps.html.

Shilts, Randy. *And the Band Played On: Politics, People, and the AIDS Epidemic*. New York, NY: St. Martin's Press, 1987.

INDEX

ABOUT THE AUTHOR

Marilee Peters grew up in Ottawa, Ontario, and one of her earliest memories is of watching an enormous children's hospital being built in the fields near her house. Ever since, she's been interested in what makes us sick, and what we can do to keep ourselves healthy.

Marilee has an MA in English literature, as well as a masters of information studies. She has written for and about non-profits in the arts, social services, and environmental fields, has worked in publishing and journalism, and for one brief but never-to-be-forgotten period of her life was employed at a subatomic physics laboratory. In *Patient Zero*, she was able to bring together her interest in writing and science.

Marilee lives in Vancouver with her husband, two children, and two cats. She is the editor of *BC Organic Grower*, a magazine for and about organic farmers in British Columbia.